5000 BRILLIANT Websites

by Geoff Preston

GW00703503

IN EASY STEPS pocket

in easy steps and **in easy steps pocket** are imprints of
Computer Step
Southfield Road . Southam . Warwickshire CV47 OFB . England
Website: www.ineasysteps.com
Email: books@ineasysteps.com

Notice of Liability

Every effort has been made to ensure that this book contains
accurate and current information. However, Computer Step and
the author shall not be liable for any loss or damage suffered by
readers as a result of any information contained herein.

Trademarks

All trademarks are acknowledged as belonging to their
respective companies.

Printed and bound in the United Kingdom

ISBN 1-84078-165-3

Contents

ReadMe.first

5 thousand from 5 billion

With an estimated 5 billion websites worldwide, the Internet is vast beyond comprehension. This book contains just over 5000, so clearly a few have been left out.

Since the Internet became available to the masses, countless people have contributed to it making it a huge fount of information to tap into. The trouble is, much of what is out there is either unsuitable or poor quality or both. This book brings together some of the best independently selected websites from around the world. You don't have to waste time ploughing through the cluttered output from search engines. This directory will get you straight to the sites you want to use.

Why this directory is better than others

There are several main approaches to the design of web directories.

Some web directories attempt to grade websites for speed or content. This book doesn't include grading of sites, which can give a false impression of a site because there are simply too many variables. Speed doesn't just depend on a site itself but also on how many people are online when the author visited the site, the speed of the author's connection (which depends on the type of connection: dial-up, ISDN, etc), the speed of the computer and the speed of the site's server. Grading of content involves very subjective decisions. For example, the author may find a website to be informative, clear, helpful, easy to use and comprehensive, but another user might find the site to be uninformative, unclear, unhelpful, difficult to use or too narrow. Also, the content on most websites changes frequently.

Other directories include lots of editorial, which takes up space resulting in fewer websites. Readers generally want to get into the site, not read a great deal about it first. Once online they can visit the site and judge it for themselves in the time it would have taken them to read the description.

There are also directories that include advertising from organisations who pay for the book to be produced. This means that the choice of websites and even categories is biased towards those that will produce more advertising revenue, rather than towards those that will be useful and entertaining for the reader.

This book avoids grading and long editorial, and is independent. The sites featured here have been carefully selected, and all of them have been tested online as near to the publication date of the book as possible, to maximise accuracy. They have been categorised to make it as easy as possible to find exactly what you want.

How to access a site

When you've located the website you're interested in, open your browser and type the address exactly as it appears in the panel labelled **Address**. When you've entered it, press the Enter or Return key and the website should be displayed.

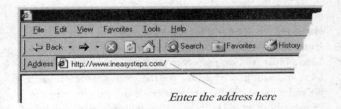

Enter the address here

What if it doesn't work?

There are over 5000 web addresses in this book and, frankly, I wouldn't be surprised if a few do not work by the time you read this. The fact is that the Internet is notoriously transient. A site that exists today may have vanished from the face of the Earth tomorrow. Many of the sites on the Internet are run by individuals who have been provided with free space to create their own website, but once the novelty has worn off, the sites are abandoned. But even large companies can run into problems.

If you enter a long address and the web page is not displayed, try deleting some of the address from the right until you get back to **.com/** or to the part that denotes the country of origin (for example **.co.uk/**). That should take you to the home page of the site from where you can navigate to the particular page referred to in the directory.

Where possible, websites by individuals have been avoided. As for the sites that no longer work, all I can say is sorry. At the time of writing, all sites referred to in this directory did work.

Help us to keep you up-to-date

If one of the websites listed here doesn't work, please let us know. Send an email to Computer Step (books@ ineasysteps.com) and let us know the page, the name and the address of the website and we will remove it in the next edition. If you stumble across sites that you think should be included, use the same email address, tell us the name of the site, the address and a brief description of what it's about.

Computer Step and the author would like to thank all the people who contributed suggestions for sites. These have been included in this edition.

Although this book was written by a British author, the majority of the sites should be of use to users across the world.

Art

This three-letter word seems to cover anything you want it to. Here, I've restricted its use to Artists and Artwork, Antiques, Ballet, Opera, Crafts and Literature.

Art Galleries

You don't have to travel the world to visit the top art galleries as most now have their own website enabling you to bring the gallery into your home. Of course, it's not really as good as visiting in person, but many of these sites are a close second.

Aberdeen Art Gallery	www.aagm.co.uk/
American Arts Guild and Gallery	www.aagg.com/
Art Gallery of New South Wales	www.artgallery.nsw.gov.au/
Art Republic	www.artrepublic.com/
Axia Modern Art	www.axiamodernart.com.au/
Courtauld Institute	www.courtauld.ac.uk/
Hayward Gallery	www.hayward-gallery.org.uk/
Louvre, The	mistral.culture.fr/louvre
Metropolitan Museum	www.metmuseum.org

Museum of Modern Art	www.moma.org
National Gallery	www.nationalgallery.org.uk/
Nat. Museum & Gallery Cardiff	www.nmgw.ac.uk/nmgc/index.en
National Portrait Gallery	www.npg.org.uk/
Norwich Gallery	www.nsad.ac.uk/gallery/
Online Art Gallery	www.artandparcel.com/
Royal Academy	www.royalacademy.org.uk/

Tate Gallery	www.tate.org.uk/
Tribal Art Dir.	www.tribalartdirectory.com/top_nav.htm
Virtual Art Gallery	www.art.net/
Wallace Collection	www.the-wallace/collection.org.uk/

Artists

When one thinks of an artist, it's invariably one of the so-called 'old-masters', many of whom have a website or two about them. But don't forget some of the more modern artists.

Artcyclopedia	www.artcyclopedia.com/
Brennan Ian	www.iangb.com/
David F Wilson	www.users.globalnet.co.uk/~dfwil/toc.htm
Feast of Leonardo	www.webgod.net/leonardo

Joyce Rowsell	**members.aol.com/rowsellj/**
LS Lowry	**www.l-s-lowry.co.uk/**
Monet's World	**www.artchive.com/artchive/M/** **monet.html**

Picasso	**http://www.artnet.com/** **magazine/features/stern/stern2-** **25-99.asp**
Pre-Victorian Artists	**www.speel.demon.co.uk/** **artist18.htm**
Victorian Artists	**www.speel.demon.co.uk/** **listart.htm**

Antiques

Personally I'm not fussed about the age of an item or its background. I would just as soon have a china teapot from the local discount store than a priceless antique that you daren't use in case it gets chipped. I recognise I'm probably in the minority, so here are a few sites from dealers and galleries.

Alliance Antiques	www.alliance-antiques.com/
Antiques For Everyone	www.sharongarberantiques.com/
Antique Shop	www.antique-shop.com
Art Deco Jewellery	www.laade.org/laade/schemes/sow3.html
Art-Co French Art Deco	www.antiquites-france.com/
Conservation and Restoration	restorationlab.com/
Daltons Antiques	www.daltons.com/
Decodealers Art Deco Directory	www.decodealers.co.uk/
Great Wall	www.greatwallantique.com/
Indian Oaks Antique Mall	www.indianoaksantiquemall.com/
J. Hill Antiques	www.jhill.com/
Jazzy Art Deco	www.jazzyartdeco.com/
Kittinger Furniture	www.kittengerfurniture.com/
Legacy Antiques and Fine Art	legacyantiques.com/index.html
Mir Antiques Antwerp	www.antiquesantwerp.com/
Modernism Gallery	www.modernism.com/
National Art Deco Fair	www.artdeco-fairs.co.uk/
Odyssey Fine Arts Ltd	www.odysseyart.co.uk/

Old Asia Gallery	www.oldasiagallery.com/
Old Bear Company	www.flair.co.uk/oldbear
Old World Art & Treasures	artreasures.com/
Otford Antiques & Collectors	www.otfordantiques.co.uk/
P.L. James & Son Antiques	www.plj-antiques.com/
Past Pleasures Antiques	www.cyberattic.com/~pleasures
Pieter Hoogendijk	www.artnet.com/phoogendijk.html
Post Road Gallery	www.postroadgallery.com/
Rhumba!	www.tace.com/rhumba
Russki	www.russiansilver.co.uk/
Sheryl's Art Deco	www.zyworld.com/shez69/sheryls-art-deco-site.htm
Tango Art Deco	www.tango-artdeco.co.uk/
Vintage Hardware	www.vintagehardware.com/
Vintage Watches	www.halem-times.com/
Weston Antiques (UK)	www.antiques-shop.co.uk/

Ballet

I'd never been to a ballet until I got inspired by some of these websites which give full details of performances. Some even allow you to book online.

American Ballet Theatre	www.abt.org/
Australian Ballet	www.australianballet.com.au/
Ballet in Russia	www.russianballet.org/

Ballet International	www.ballet-tanz.de/
Ballet.co	www.ballet.co.uk/
Bolshoi Theater	www.alincom.com/bolshoi/
City Ballet of London	freespace.virgin.net/ david.browne/cbl.htm
Continental Ballet Company	www.continentalballet.com/
Electric Ballerina	www.novia.net/~jlw/electric/ electric.html
English National Ballet	www.ballet.org.uk/
Kirov Ballet and Academy	www.kirovballet.com/
London Junior Ballet	www.londonjuniorballet.cwc.net/
Moscow Flying Ballet	www.flying-ballet.com/
National Ballet of Canada	www.national.ballet.ca/
New York City Ballet	www.nycballet.com/
Royal Ballet School	www.royal-ballet-school.org.uk/
Russian Classical Ballet	www.aha.ru/~vladmo/
Sadler's Wells	www.sadlers-wells.com/
Scottish Ballet	www.scottishballet.co.uk/

Crafts

I wasn't sure whether to put these sites here or in the section on hobbies. I don't suppose it really matters, but if you like doing something arty/crafty, or would like to learn about a particular craft, there's a good selection here.

| Africa Warehouse | www.ishop.co.uk/ishop/62 |
| Arts & Crafts Society | www.arts-crafts.com/ |

Art Resources	www.artresources.com/
Black Ash	basketry.miningco.com/library/weekly/aa111698.htm
Candleshop	www.candleshop.com/
Candles and Supplies.com	www.candlesandsupplies.com/
Candle Supply.com	www.candlesupply.com/
Card Inspirations	www.cardinspirations.co.uk/
Ceramic Art Space	www.ceramicartspace.com/
China Painting	www.geocities.com/Paris/3543/
Clock Movements	www.clockmovements.com/
Country Seat Inc., The	www.countryseat.com/
Crafts Etc!	www.craftsetc.com/
Crafts for Kids	craftsforkids.about.com/kids/craftsforkids/mbody.htm
Crochet 'n' More	crochetnmore.com/
Crochet Musings	crochet.rpmdp.com/
Crochet	crochet.miningco.com/index.htm
Crochet Guild Of America	www.crochet.org/
Designer Stencil	www.designerstencils.com/
Enamels	www.enamelist.com/
Fascinating Folds	fascinating-folds.com/
Fusion Art Glass	www.fusionartglass.com/
Glass Art Society	www.glassart.org/
Glass Craftsman	www.artglassworld.com/
Glass Museum	www.glass.co.nz/
Green Dragon	www.greendragon.co.uk/

Heart Bead	www.heartbead.com/
Hexaflexagons	www.xnet.com/~aak/hexahexa.html
Kids Kits Crafts and Projects	www.kidskitscrafts.com/
Knitting Knook	www.yarnshop.com/
Knitting Now	www.knittingnow.com/
Knitting Today	www.knittingtoday.com/
Lace Language	www.touchoflace.com/
Lace Magazine Home Page	www.lacemagazine.com/
Lacis	www.lacis.com/
Lampwork Flamework Glass Art	www.mickelsenstudios.com/
Mad Stencilist	www.madstencilist.com/
Morrison Glass Art	www.eskimo.com/~kmc/mga.htm
OrigamiUSA	www.origami-usa.org/
Painted Fire	www.seattle2000.com/paintedfire/
Paperfolding.com	www.paperfolding.com/
Southwest Stencils	www.swstencils.com/
Stenciling.com	www.stenciling.co.uk/
Stencil Library	www.stencil-library.com/
Vogue Knitting	www.vogueknitting.com/
Wax House, The	www.waxhouse.com/
Wonderful World of Crochet	www.tallassee.net/~crafts/cro1.htm

Literature

The pen is mightier than the sword and over the years there have been many great men and women who have wielded it to great effect.

Booker Prize, The	www.bookerprize.co.uk/
Edward Lear Home Page	edwardlear.tripod.com/
George Eliot	www.kirjasto.sci.fi/gelliot.htm
Jane Austen	www.pemberley.com/janeinfo/janeinfo.html
Jonathan Swift	www.mala.bc.ca/~mcneil/
Kipling Society	www.kipling.org.uk/
Milton-L Home Page, The	www.urich.edu/~creamer/milton/
Oscar Wilde	www.poetrytodayonline.com/cp.html
Robert Louis Stevenson	www.unibg.it/rls/rls.htm
Walter Scott, Sir	www.mastertexts.com/scott_sir_walter
William Shakespeare	the-tech.mit.edu/shakespeare/works.html
William Thackeray	www.incompetech.com/authors/thackeray/

Opera

Apparently there is a storyline, but it's totally incomprehensible.

English National Opera	www.eno.org/

New York City Opera	**www.nycopera.com/**
Opera Now	**www.rhinegold.co.uk/ rgmgon1.cfm**
Opera Stuff	**www.columbia.edu/~km34/ sing.html**
Opera World	**www.operaworld.com/**
OperaWeb	**www.opera.it/english/ operaweb.html**

Royal Opera House	**www.royalopera.org/**
Sadler's Wells	**www.sadlers-wells.com/**
Sydney Opera House	**www.soh.nsw.gov.au/**
Sydney Opera House Virtual Tour	**www.oznet.net.au/opera**
Virtual Opera House	**www.opera.co.za/**

Books

Whatever your taste in reading matter, you'll find it on the Internet.

Bookstores

Whenever I visit a particular high street bookshop (which isn't very often actually) I'm always amazed that the staff allow customers to read the books and papers. Having a quick look at the plot is one thing, but some people actually sit down and read the book and then leave without buying it. The advantage of buying at an online bookshop is that the book you get will be new, unread and unthumbed. The corners won't be 'dog-eared' and the spine won't be broken which means you can give it as a gift without the recipient thinking you've raided your own bookcase.

Absolutely Weird Bookshelf	www.strangewords.com/
Advanced Book Exchange	www.abebooks.com/
Alibris	www.alibris.com/
Alphabet Street	www.alphabetstreet.co.uk/
Amazon	www.amazon.co.uk/

Art2Art	www.art2art.com/
Audio Book Club	www.audiobookclub.com/
Barnes and Noble	www.barnesandnoble.com/
B.T.Batsford	www.batsford.com/
Bibliofind	www.bibliofind.com/

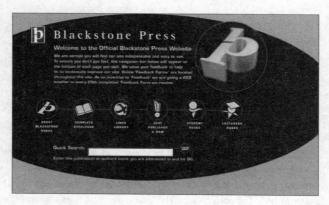

Blackstone Press	www.blackstonepress.co.uk/
Blackwells	bookshop.blackwell.co.uk/
BOL	www.bol.com/
Book Garden, The	www.bookgarden.com/
Book People, The	www.thebookpeople.co.uk/
Book Pl@ce, The	www.thebookplace.com/
Booklovers	www.booklovers.co.uk/
BookNook	www.booknook.com/

Books A Million	www.booksamillion.com/
Books are Magic	www.booksaremagic.com/
Books for a Better Life	www.msnyc.org/books/bblindex.htm
Bookstreet, 1	www.1bookstreet.com/
Brattle Book Shop	www.brattlebookshop.com/
Chapters	www.chapters.ca/
Children's Book Centre	www.childrensbookcentre.co.uk/
Children's Bookshop, The	www.childrensbookshop.com/
Computer Books Online	www.computerbooksonline.com/
Computer Manuals	www.compman.co.uk/
Country Bookshop	www.countrybookshop.co.uk/
Dymocks	www.dymocks.com.au/
English Book Centre	www.ebcoxford.co.uk/
Funorama	www.funorama.com/
Internet Bookshop	www.bookshop.co.uk/
James Thin Booksellers	www.jamesthin.co.uk/
John Smith & Son Bookshops	www.johnsmith.co.uk/
Lion Publishing	www.lion-publishing.co.uk/
Long Barn Books	www.longbarnbooks.co.uk/
Macmillan Computer Books	www.mcp.com/
Maps Worldwide	www.mapsworldwide.co.uk/
Millennium Books	www.meridian-experience.com/
Mulberry Bush, The	www.mulberrybush.com/
Ottakar's	www.ottakars.co.uk/

Oxford University Press	**www.oup.co.uk/**
Pan Macmillan	**www.panmacmillan.com/**
PC Bookshops	**www.pcbooks.co.uk/**
Pickabook	**www.pickabook.co.uk/**
Powell's	**powells.com/**
Red House	**www.redhouse.co.uk/**
Richard Nicholson of Chester	**www.antiquemaps.com/**
San Diego Technical Books	**www.booksmatter.com/**
Saxons	**www.saxons.co.uk/**
Scholar's Bookshelf, The	**www.scholarsbookshelf.com/**
Sci-Fi	**www.sci-fi.co.uk/**
Sportspages	**www.sportspages.co.uk/**
Tesco	**www.tesco.co.uk/books**
Varsity Books	**www.varsitybooks.com/**
Virgin Books	**www.virgin-books.com/**
Waterstones	**www.waterstones.co.uk/**
WH Smith	**www.whsmith.co.uk/**

Publishers

Some publishers sell their books on the web, but even those who don't carry full details of their books and outlets where you can purchase them.

Addison Wesley Longman	**www.awl.com/**
Blackwell	**www.blackwellpublishers.co.uk/**
Butterworths	**www.butterworths.co.uk/**

Cambridge University Press   www.cup.cam.ac.uk/

Computer Step (in easy steps)	www.ineasysteps.com/
DC Thomson	www.dcthomson.co.uk/
Dorling Kindersley	www.dk.com/
Ferry Publications	www.ferrypubs.co.uk/
Ginn	www.ginn.co.uk/
Harper Collins	www.harpercollins.co.uk/
HMSO	www.hmso.gov.uk/
Hodder & Stoughton	www.hodder.co.uk/
Kogan Page	www.kogan-page.co.uk/
Macmillan	www.macmillan.co.uk/
McGraw-Hill	www.mcgraw-hill.co.uk/
No Exit Press	www.noexit.co.uk/
Ocean Press & Publishing Ltd	www.ocean-press.com/ocean/
Paragon	www.paragon.co.uk/

Pearson	www.pearson.co.uk/
Penguin	www.penguin.co.uk/
Puffin	www.puffin.co.uk/
Random House	www.randomhouse.co.uk/
Reed	www.reedbusiness.com/
Sunstone Press Book Publishers	www.sunstonepress.com

Thames and Hudson	www.thameshudson.co.uk/
Thistle Press	www.thistlepress.co.uk/
Thompson	www.thompson.com/

Business

Modern life seems to require professional assistance like never before.

Accountants

A & N Chartered Accountants	www.aruna.com/
Accountants Directory	www.hampshire.businesslink.co.uk/accountants/
Accountants thru' Internet	www.netaccountants.com/
Ainsworths	www.ainsworths.co.uk/
Alfred Green Partnership	www.agp-accountants.co.uk/
Andrews & Co.	www.andrews-accountants.co.uk/
Association of Chartered Certified Accountants (ACCA)	www.acca.org.uk/
Axelsen Mills	www.aml-accountants.co.uk/
Butler & Co	www.butler-co.com/
Demacks Chartered Accountants	www.demack.co.uk/
Glazers Chartered Accountants	www.glazers.co.uk/
ECP	www.ecpaccountants.co.uk/
Hillier Hopkins	www.hillier-hopkins.co.uk/

Hooks Chartered Accountants	www.hooks.co.uk/
ICAEW	www.icaew.co.uk/
Institute of Chartered Accountants of Scotland	www.icas.org.uk/
International Association of Practising Accountants	www.iapa-accountants.com/
Jayson Newman	www.jayson-newman.com/
Kellys Chartered Accountants	www.kellys.uk.co/
Ken F Forsyth Accountants	www.kenforsyth.com/
Kingcott Accountants	www.kingcott.co.uk/
Kingswood Chartered Accountants	www.kingswood.org.uk/
Limehouse & Co.	www.limehouse-accountants.co.uk/
Mitchells Chartered Accountants	www.mitchells.org/
Morris & Co.	www.moco.co.uk/
Randall & Payne	www.randall-payne.co.uk/
Robinson	www.robinson-chartered-accountants.co.uk/
Russell Heath	www.russellheath.co.uk/
Spofforths Chartered Accountants	www.spofforths.co.uk/
Sterlings Chartered Accountants	www.sterlings.co.uk/
Winters Chartered Accountants	www.winters.co.uk/

Advertising Agencies

Advertising Association	www.adassoc.org.uk/
AdWeb Ltd	www.adweb.co.uk/
Alphabet Advertising	www.alphabet-ic.com/
Bartle Bogle Hegarty	www.bbh.co.uk/
Creative Partnership	www.creativepartnership.co.uk/
Doremus	www.doremus.com/
Dowell & Associates	www.dowell.co.uk/
Grey Worldwide	www.grey.co.uk/
Institute of Practitioners in Advertising	www.ipa.co.uk/
ISBA	www.isba.org.uk/

J Walter Thompson	www.jwtworld.com/

Leagas Delaney	www.leagasdelaney.com/
Leith Agency	www.leith.co.uk/
Levy McCallum Advertising Agency	www.levymccallum.co.uk/
Lowe Live	www.lowelive.com/
MAP	www.map-plc.co.uk/
McCann-Erickson	www.mccann-belfast.com/
MediaTel	www.mediatel.co.uk/
New Horizons	www.newhorizons.co.uk/
Nicholson's Advertising Ltd	www.nicholson-advertising.co.uk/
Publicis	www.publicis.co.uk/
RDW Advertising	www.rdw-advertising.co.uk/
Saatchi & Saatchi	www.saatchi-saatchi.com/
Union, The	www.union.co.uk/
WKL Advertising & Design	www.wkl.co.uk/
World Writers	www.worldwriters.com/
WPP Group plc	www.wpp.com/wpp/

Chambers of Commerce

British Chambers of Commerce	www.britishchambers.org.uk/
Ely & White CofC	www.elynevada.org/
Essex CofC	www.essexchambers.co.uk/
Glasgow CofC	www.glasgowchamber.org/
Hanover Area CofC	www.hanoverchamber.com/
Hertfordshire CofC	www.hertschamber.com/
Hull and Humber CofC	www.hull-humber-chamber.co.uk/

Lancaster CofC	www.lancaster-chamber.org.uk/
North Staffordshire CofC	www.northstaffs-chamber.co.uk/
Nottinghamshire CofC	www.nottschamber.co.uk/
Southampton and Fareham CofC	www.soton-chamber.co.uk/
Wayne County CofC	www.waynecountycc.com/
Wessex Association of Chambers of Commerce	www.wessexchambers.org.uk/

Couriers

Business is picking up for carriers now that online shopping is so easy.

A&M Transport Services	www.amtransport.co.uk/
A–Z Worldwide Airfreight Directory	www.azairfreight.co.uk/
AIMS Logistics	www.aimseurope.com/
Ayr Despatch	www.ayrdespatch.com/
Branson	www.bransoncourier.com/
Businesspost	www.business-post.com/
CCS	www.ccscouriers.co.uk/
Courier Systems	www.couriersystems.co.uk/
Courier Insurance	www.courierinsurance.co.uk/
Dataline Express	www.dataline-express.co.uk/
Deadline Despatch	www.deadline.co.uk/
DHL	www.dhl.co.uk/
Excel	www.excel.co.uk/

Excel Courier Services	www.excelcourierservices.com/
Export	www.exportcourier.co.uk/
Federal Express	www.fedex.com/
Greyhound	www.greyhound-couriers.co.uk/
IAATC	www.aircourier.co.uk/
Link-Up Carriers	www.link-up-carriers.co.uk/

NIGHTFREIGHT

Services   Contacts   Investor Information   Download Area   Recruitment   Transport Training

Nightfreight plc

Night-Trak
Proof of delivery
tracking service

Arrange a Collection

Organise a re-delivery

Contact

Postcode Search

News Flash
Management buy
Nightfreight- Update
Click for details

Express Parcel Freight

Logistic Fulfilment

Ocean & Air Freight

European Freight

Transport Training

Tank Containers

Express Parcel Freight

Through our network of 51 depots we can collect and deliver parcel freight of any size and shape to and from any point within the UK and Ireland. Our next day service can be enhanced to deliver before 9:30am or before Noon or we can offer a more leisurely 48 hour delivery service

Please use the links at the top of the screen to navigate around the site.

Nightfreight plc	www.nightfreight.co.uk/
On The Dot	www.onthedot.co.uk/
One-Stop Parcel Tracking	www.upgradecity.com/ tracking.htm
Parcel Force	www.parcelforce.com/
Parcel Recovery Service	www.parcelrecovery.com
Parcel2go.com	www.parcel2go.com/
Pegasus	www.pegasus-couriers.com/

Securicor plc	www.securicor.co.uk/
Speed	www.speed.co.uk/
Speed Courier Worldwide	www.mcb.net/scw/
TNT	www.tnt.co.uk/
Total Courier Systems	www.tcs.freeuk.com/
UPS	www.ups.com/
World Courier	www.worldcourier.com/

Solicitors

Amhurst Brown Colombotti	www.abc-solicitors.com/
Barnett Alexander Chart	www.bac-solicitors.co.uk/
Boyes Turner & Burrows	www.btb-solicitors.co.uk/
Clarks	www.clarks-solicitors.co.uk/
Compensation Solicitors Online	www.compensationsolicitors-online.com/
Crown Prosecution Service	www.cps.gov.uk/
Edward Lewis Solicitors	www.edwardlewis.co.uk/
Hilliers Solicitors	www.hilliers-solicitors.co.uk/
Law Society	www.lawsociety.org.uk/
Law Society of England and Wales	www.lawsoc.org.uk/
Law Society of Scotland	www.lawscot.org.uk/
Ludgates	www.ludgates-solicitors.co.uk/
Macpherson & Kelley Solicitors	www.mk.com.au/
Shoosmiths Solicitors	www.shoosmiths-solicitors.co.uk/

Solicitors for Independent Financial Advice www.sifa.co.uk/

Stewarts Solicitors www.stewarts-solicitors.co.uk/

UK Legal – Solicitors Index www.uklegal.com/solicito/

Veitch Penny Solicitors www.veitchpenny.co.uk/

Wilkins Solicitors www.wilkins-solicitors.co.uk/

Trade Associations

Aluminium Federation www.alfed.org.uk/

Association of Independent Music www.musicindie.org/

Association of Photographers www.aophoto.co.uk/

British Agricultural & Garden Machinery Association www.bagma.com/

British Box & Packaging Association www.boxpackaging.org.uk/

British Constructional Steelwork Association (BCSA) www.bcsa.org.uk/

British Interactive Multimedia Association www.bima.co.uk/

British Security Industry Association www.bsia.co.uk/

British Toy & Hobby Association www.btha.co.uk/

British Woodworking Federation (BWF) www.bwf.org.uk/

Building Societies Association www.bsa.org.uk/

CSSA www.cssa.co.uk/

Electrical Contractors Association **www.eca.co.uk/**

Food and Drink Federation **www.fdf.org.uk/**

Freight Transport Association **www.fta.co.uk/**

Glass and Glazing Federation **www.ggf.org.uk/**

House Builders Federation **www.hbf.co.uk/**

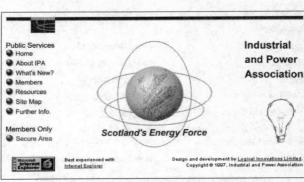

Public Services
- Home
- About IPA
- What's New?
- Members
- Resources
- Site Map
- Further Info.

Members Only
- Secure Area

Industrial and Power Association

Scotland's Energy Force

Best experienced with Internet Explorer

Design and development by Logical Innovations Limited.
Copyright © 1997, Industrial and Power Association

Industrial and Power Association **www.ipa-scotland.org.uk/**

Music Industries Association **www.mia.org.uk/**

National Association of Estate Agents **www.naea.co.uk/**

National Association of Master Bakers **www.masterbakers.co.uk/**

Paper Industry Technical Association **www.yell.co.uk/sites/paper-ita/**

UK Forest Products Association **www.ukfpa.co.uk/**

UK Steel Association **www.uksteel.org.uk/**

| Society for British Aerospace Companies | www.sbac.co.uk/ |

Trade Unions

Commonwealth Trade Union Council	www.commonwealthtuc.org/
European Trade Union Confederation	www.etuc.org/
Equity	www.equity.org.uk/
GFTU	www.gftu.org.uk/
GMB	www.gmb.org.uk/
GMB Trade Union	www.gmbunion.org/
Trades Union Congress	www.tuc.org.uk/
Union of Construction, Allied Trades and Technicians	www.ucatt.org.uk/
Unions on the Web	www.aflcio.org/unionand.htm

| UNISON | www.unison.org.uk/ |
| Wales TUC | www.wtuc.org.uk/ |

Charities

Although not all of these sites are actually registered charities, they all set out to help those less fortunate.

Health

These charities help fight a particular disease, care for people suffering from it or raise its profile. Or all three.

Action for Blind People	www.afbp.org/
Action on Smoking and Health	www.ash.org.uk/
Age Concern	www.ace.org.uk/
Alcohol Counselling & Prevention Services	www.vois.org.uk/acaps/
Alzheimer's Disease	www.alzheimers.org.uk/
Anthony Nolan Bone Marrow Trust	www.anthonynolan.com/
Association for International Cancer Research	www.aicr.org.uk/
Barnardos	www.barnardos.org.uk/
Breast Cancer Campaign	www.bcc-uk.org/

British Heart Foundation	**www.bhf.org.uk/**
British Red Cross Society	**www.redcross.org.uk/**
CancerHelp UK	**medweb.bham.ac.uk/cancerhelp/**
Down's Syndrome Assoc., The	**www.dsa-uk.com/**
Flying Doctor	**www.rfds.org.au/**
Handicap International	**www.globalassistance.org/**
Hearing Concern	**web.ukonline.co.uk/ hearing.concern**

Help the Aged	**www.helptheaged.org.uk/**
Leukaemia Research Fund	**www.leukaemia-research.org.uk/**
Macmillan	**www.macmillan.org.uk/**
Marie Curie	**www.mariecurie.org.uk/**
Marie Stopes International	**www.mariestopes.org.uk/ index.html**

M. E. Association	glaxocentre.merseyside.org/mea.html
Multiple Sclerosis Soc	glaxocentre.merseyside.org/mss.html
Muscular Dystrophy Campaign	www.muscular-dystrophy.org/
National AIDS Trust	www.nat.org.uk/
Nat Soc. Prevention of Cruelty to Children	www.nspcc.org.uk/
Royal Nat. Institute for the Blind	www.rnib.org.uk/
Royal Society for Mentally Handicapped Children and Adults	www.mencap.org.uk/
Save the Children Fund	www.savethechildren.org.uk/

Humanitarian

There are a great many organisations which provide international support to those less well off than ourselves.

Amnesty International	www.amnesty.org.uk/
British Refugee Council	www.gn.apc.org/brcslproject
Christian Aid	www.christian-aid.org.uk/
Creating Hope International	www.creatinghope.org/
Disaster Training International	www.disastertraining.org/
East Meets West Foundation	www.eastmeetswest.org/
Friends of the Earth	www.foe.co.uk/index.html
HOPE Worldwide	www.hopeww.org/
IOBG Humanitarian Foundation	www.iobghf.org/

Oxfam   www.oxfam.org.uk/

Salvation Army   www.salvationarmy.org.uk/

Samaritans   www.samaritans.org.uk/

Sightsavers   www.sightsavers.co.uk/

Voluntary Service Overseas   www.vso.org.uk/

Women's Commission for   www.intrescom.org/wcrwc.html
Refugees

World Care   www.worldcare.org/

Organisations

Whether it be raising awareness of environmental issues or providing
help for underprivileged kids, someone, somewhere is ready to
help.

A Way Out   www.awayout.twooffice.com/

Anne Frank Educational   www.afet.org.uk/

Association of Blind Piano Tuners	www.uk-piano.org/abpt
Association of Medical Research	www.amrc.org.uk/
Breakthrough	www.breakthrough-dhi.org.uk/
British Youth Council	www.byc.org.uk/
Charity Net	www.charitynet.org/
Citizens Advice Bureau	www.poptel.org.uk/cab/
Donkey Sanctuary, The	www.thedonkeysanctuary.org.uk/
Duke of Edinburgh's Award	www.sonnet.co.uk/dea/
Gingerbread	www.gingerbread.org.uk/
Global Assistance	www.globalassistance.org/
Greenpeace	www.greenpeace.org/
Guide Star	www.guidestar.org/
I Give.com	www.igive.com/
InterAction	www.interaction.org/
International Rescue Committee	www.intrescom.org/
LifeNets	www.lifenets.org/
MESA	www.mesa.org/
National Canine Defence League	www.eurosolve.com/charity/ncdl/
Netaid	www.netaid.org/
Operation Mercy	www.mercy.t.se/
Parrot Line	www.parrotline.org/
Rotary Club	www.rotary.org/
Round Table	www.interads.co.uk/rtbi/ wokingham/
Royal Botanic Gardens	www.rbgkew.org.uk/

Royal British Legion	www.britishlegion.org.uk/
Royal National Lifeboat Institution	www.rnli.org.uk/
RSPB	www.rspb.org.uk/
Scope	www.scope.org.uk/
St John Ambulance	www.stjohnambulance.org.uk/

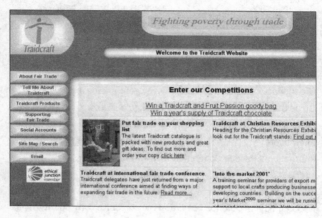

Traidcraft Exchange	www.traidcraft.co.uk/
Vegetarian Society	www.vegsoc.org/
Women's Institute	www.nfwi.org.uk/
World Foundation for Humanity	www.worldfoundation.com/
World Wildlife Fund	www.panda.org/
YMCA	www.ymca.org.uk/
Youth Hostelling Association	www.yha.org.uk/

Clothes

Virtually all of the stores here sell clothes directly to the public. Look out for those that offer free carriage as these charges can wipe out the saving made on the actual garment.

Women's Clothes

Why is it that my wife's wardrobe is four times the size of mine (not including the bulging sides) and yet I still get a daily rendition of 'I don't know what to wear?' followed closely by 'I don't have anything to wear'.

Abercrombie & Fitch	www.abercrombie.com/
Access Style	www.accessstyle.com/
Advantage Discount Bridal	www.advantagebridal.com/
African Imports	www.african-import.com/
Agnes.com	www.agnes.com/
Allola Cashmere Fashion Shop	www.allola.net/
Alternative Gowns	www.alt-gowns.com/
Angels-sexy-bikini.com	www.angels-sexy-bikini.com/
Angelwear	angelwearhawaii.com/

Ann 'N' Eve Collection	www.annneve.com/
April Cornell	www.aprilcornell.com/
Artigiano	www.artigiano.com/
Baa Baa Zuzu	www.baabaazuzu.com/
Bainbridge & Boston	www.bainbridge.co.uk/
Bargain Clothing Corporation	www.bargainclothing.com/
Basement Clothing USA	www.BasementClothing.com/
Batik Center	www.batikcenter.bizland.com/
Bebe	www.bebe.com/
Beme.com	www.beme.com/
Benetton Online	www.benettononline.com/
Best Bridesmaid	www.bestbridesmaid.com/
Best Prom Dresses	www.bestpromdresses.com/
Black Frock	www.blackfrock.com/
Blacktiegown	www.blacktiegown.com/
Bloomingdales	www.bloomingdales.com/
Bluefly.com	www.bluefly.com/
Bo Bo Boutique	www.boboboutique.com/
Bodysuit.com	www.bodysuit.com/
BodyTape Inc	www.bodytape.com/
Boston Proper	www.bostonproper.com/
Bras Direct	www.brasdirect.co.uk/
Bridal Creations	www.bridalcreations.com/
Bridal Marketplace	www.bridalmarketplace.com/
Bridesmaids.com	www.bridesmaids.com/

Burlington Coat Factory	www.burlingtoncoatfactory.com/
Buy In America	www.buyinamerica.com/
Cameo Lingerie	www.cameolingerie.com/
Capecrest.com	www.capecrest.com/
Caro Fashion-Design	www.caro-modedesign.de/
Carushka	www.carushka.com/
Cashmere Company	www.cashmerecompany.com/
Chadwick's of Boston	www.chadwicks.com/
Chelsea Nites	www.chelseanites.com/
Chic Ladies Fashions	www.chicfashions.co.uk/
Ciciriello	www.ciciriello.com/
Clothes Heaven	www.clothesheaven.com/
Clothing Connection	www.clothingconnection.co.uk/
Clothesnet.com	www.clothesnet.com/
Club Lace Catalog	www.clublace.com/
Club Monaco	www.clubmonaco.com/
Coat Factory	www.freewayfashions.com/
Coldwater Creek	www.coldwatercreek.com/
Cool Girls Japan	www.coolgirlsjapan.com/
Cotton Clothing Co	www.cottonclothingco.com/
Couture Online	www.coutureon-line.com/
Crystal Tease	www.crystaltease.com/
Curves.com	www.curves.com/
CXD	www.cxdlondon.com/
CybernetPlaza.com	www.cybernetplaza.com/

D Terrell Ltd	www.dterrell.com/
Dahle's Big & Tall	www.dahles-bigandtall.com/
Daisy Nook Designs	www.daisynook.co.uk/
Dalton Designs	www.daltondesigns.com/
Daytona Thunderwear	daytonathunderwear.com/
Decadestwo	www.decadestwo.com/
Delia's	www.delias.com/
Denim Designs	www.denimdesigns.com/
Designer Exposure	www.designerexposure.com/
Dia knitwear	www.diaknitwear.com/
Diesel	www.diesel.com/
DiFrancia Designer Garters	www.difrancia.com/
Discreetness Lingerie	www.discreetness.com/ discreetness/catalog/plusize.html
Donna Karan	www.firstview.com/designerlist/ donnakaran.html
Dorothy Perkins	www.dorothyperkins.co.uk/
eArmoire	www.earmoire.com/
Easyshop	www.easyshop.co.uk/
Eddie Bauer Online Store	www.eddiebauer.com/
Egowns.com	www.egowns.com/
Elsahaag	www.elsahaag.co.uk/
Emans Atelier	www.emansatelier.com/
Enokiworld	www.enokiworld.com/
Escapeze Fashions	www.escapeze.com/
Esprit	www.esprit.com/

Evans	www.evans.ltd.uk/
Eveningbag.com	www.eveningbag.com/
Evening Store	www.theeveningstore.com/
Fantasy Apparel	www.fantasyapparel.com/
Fantasy Plus Fashions	www.fantasyplus.com/
Fashion Dish	www.fashiondish.com/
Fashion Junkie	www.fashionjunkie.com/
Fashionmall.com	www.fashionmall.com/
FASHIonLINE	www.fashionline.co.at/english/index_english.html
Fashion Victim Women's Tees	www.fashionvictim.com/
Fashionmine	www.fashionmine.com/
Fat Face	www.fatface.co.uk/
Father Nature's Boutique	www.fathernature.com/
FCUK	www.frenchconnection.com/
Filene's Basement	www.filenesbasement.com/
Fine Things	www.fine-things.net/
FK Company	www.fkcompany.com/
Formal Fashions	www.formalfashions.com/
Fun Fashions Inc.	www.funfashions.com/
Gad Abouts International	www.gad-abouts.com/
Galleria Mall Online	www.galleriamallonline.com/
Gap	www.gap.com/
G.H. Bass & Co.	www.ghbass.com/
Ghost	www.ghost.co.uk/
Girlshop	www.girlshop.com/

Graffiti Online	www.graffitionline.com/
Grand Style Women's Club	www.grandstyle.com/cloth03.htm
Gurlwear	www.gurlwear.com/
Haburi.com	www.haburi.com/
Hampton Point	www.hamptonpoint.com/
Hanes Her Way	www.hanesherwaybras.com/
Harebell	www.harebell.com/
Harolds	www.harolds.com/
Holiday Halters	www.holidayhalters.com/
Hummingbird Activewear	www.hummingbirdwear.com/
In The Nik Fashions	www.itn.uss.net.au/
Isabella Bird	www.isabellabird.com/
Itsybits.com	www.itsybits.com/
J. Jill	www.jjill.com/
JoJo Maman Bebe	www.jojomamanbebe.co.uk/
Jordache	www.jordache.com/
Judy Parker Hand Knit & Crochet	www.judyknits.com/
Kasper ASL	www.kasper.com/
Katwalk Fashion Showroom	www.thekatwalk.com/
Kays	www.kaysnet.com/
Kendall Creek Collections	www.kendallcreek.com/
Knitwear Boutique of Builth Wells	www.midwales.co.uk/knitwear/
LadyBug Originals	www.ladybugoriginals.com/
LadyBwear.com	www.ladybwear.com/
Lands' End	www.landsend.com/

Lane Bryant	www.lanebryant.com/
Lapetina	www.lapetina.com/
Le Galleria	www.dchee.com/
Leftgear.com	www.leftgear.com/
Leila	www.leilaclothing.com/
Leotard Company	www.tlcsport.co.uk
Lilly Pulitzer	www.lillyshop.com/
Lingerie At Large	lingerieatlarge.com/
Little House Fashions	www.littlehousefashions.com/
Loehmann's	www.loehmanns.com/
Long Tall Clothing Company	www.tallwomensclothing.com/
Macy's	www.macys.com/
Mandee	www.mandee.com/
Maple Drive Fine Lingerie	www.lingerie.co.uk/
Marge Rohrer	handwovenstylesbymarge.com/
Marks & Spencer	www.marksandspencer.com/index.html
Mauriziotoscani	www.mauriziotoscani.com/
Max Studio	www.maxstudio.com/
Meena Bazar	www.meenabazar.com/
Moms At Play	momsatplay.com/
Montage/Double Take	www.montagedt.com/
Nellie M. Boutique	www.nelliem.com/
New Natalies Bridals	www.newnataliesbridals.com/
Newbury Bond	www.newburybond.com/

Newport News	www.newport-news.com/
Niftythreads.com	www.niftythreads.com/
Nike Europe	www.nike.com/europe/
Nordstrom	store.nordstrom.com/
NY Dress Co	www.nydressco.com/
Nygård International	www.nygard.com/
OneHanesPlace	www.onehanesplace.com/
Pagan Playground	www.paganplayground.com/
Peach Berserk	www.peachberserk.com/

Peruvian Connection	www.peruvianconnection.com/
Petitediva.com	www.petitediva.com/
Pick up 'n' Go	www.pickupngo.com/
Principles	www.principles.co.uk/
Prom-dresses.com	www.prom-dresses.com/
Promod Shop	www.promodshop.com/

PunPun	www.punpun.com/
Purpleskirt.com	www.purpleskirt.com/
Pzaz.com	www.pzaz.com/
Quinceanera	www.dressesbylilia.com/
Rivetwear	www.rivetwear.com/
Robyn Boyd	www.robynboyd.com.au/
Rolli-Moden	www.rolli-moden.com/
Roots	www.roots.com/
S. Robin	www.srobin.com/
Sara Boutique	www.saraboutique.com/
Sarah's	www.sarahs-clothes.com/
Scarves, Silk and Art	art-and-scarves.com/
Selective	www.selective.co.uk/
Shop at Anna	www.shopatanna.com/
Sila	www.sila.com/
Simply Dresses	www.simplydresses.com/
Simply Elegant Boutique	www.simplyelegantboutique.com/
Sisley	www.sisley.com/
Skirts and Shirts.com	www.skirtsandshirts.com/
Sky David Park	www.skydavidpark.com/
Sophies Circle	www.sophiescircle.com/
SoYouWanna Dress Better	www.soyouwanna.com/
Sparkle Plenty Fashions	www.sparkleplenty-fashions.com/
Style Society	www.stylesociety.com/
StyleShop Direct	www.styleshopdirect.com/

Syms Clothing	www.syms.com/index.html
Tall Etc.	www.tallwomen.com/
Territory Ahead	www.territoryahead.com/
Theme	www.themesingapore.com/
Tianello	www.tianello.com/
Tiaraworld	www.tiaraworld.com/
Timberland	www.timberland.com/
Time For Prom	www.timeforprom.com/
Title Nine Sports	www.title9sports.com/
TJ Formal	www.tjformal.com/
Top Shop	www.tops.co.uk/
Unique Wedding	www.uniquewedding.com/
Unusual Knits	www.maguirecustomknits.com/
Uuma.com	www.uuma.com/
Veilnet.com	www.veilnet.com/
Very Tall Women	www.verytallwomen.com/
VioletPeace	www.violetpeace.com/
Wicked Kitten	www.wickedkitten.com/
Wild Women Enterprises	wildwomen-ent.com/
Winona	www.winona.com/
Womensuits.com	www.womensuits.com/
Wonderbra	www.wonderbrausa.com/
World Piece	www.world-piece.com/
YOOX	www.yoox.co.uk/
Zona Boutique	www.zonaclothes.com/

Men's Clothes

To demonstrate the previous point, there are fewer sites here for men's clothes than for women's clothes. But only just.

2002 Ties.com	www.2002ties.com/
Absolute Ties	absoluteties.com/
African Imports	www.african-import.com/
Allmensunderwear.com	www.allmensunderwear.com/
Aloha Hawaiian shirts	alohahawaiianshirts.com/
Alohaland	www.alohaland.com/
America's Shirt Catalogue	www.hugestore.com/
American Male and Company	www.american-male.com/
Antigua Group, Inc	www.antiguasportswear.com/
As Ties Go By	www.astiesgoby.com/
AUkdesignershop	www.ukdesignershop.com/
Banana Republic	www.bananarepublic.com/
Bavender	www.bavender.com/
Bespoke Tailors	www.menswear.ie/
Big and Tall Guys	www.bigandtallguys.com/home.html
Blackman Custom Tailor	www.blackmantailor.com/
Bluefly.com	www.bluefly.com/
BMG Imports	www.bmgimports.com/
Boston Bow Tie	www.bostonbowtie.com/
Bow Tie Club	www.bowtieclub.com/
Boxer Rebellion	www.boxerrebellion.com/

Bromleys	www.shirts-direct.co.uk/
Brooks Brothers	www.brooks-brothers.net/
Burlington Coat Factory	www.burlingtoncoatfactory.com/
Burton	www.burtonmenswear.co.uk/
Buy Ties	www.buyties.com/
Cafe Coton Menswear	www.cafecoton.co.uk/
Captain's Closet	www.captainscloset.com/
Chadwick's of Boston	www.chadwicks.com/
Charles Tyrwhitt	www.ctshirts.co.uk/
City Boxers	www.cityboxers.com/
Classic Kit	www.classickit.com/
Clothing Guy	www.clothingguy.com/
Clothes Store	www.the-clothes-store.com/
Clothesnet.com	www.clothesnet.com/mens.htm
Clothing Connection	www.clothingconnection.co.uk/
Clothing.net	www.clothing.net/
Corsair Ties	www.corsairties.com/
Countess Mara	www.countessmaraties.com/
Cowboy Corral	www.cowboycorral.com/
Dahle's Big & Tall	www.dahles-bigandtall.com/
Dalton Reade	www.daltonreade.com/
D'Angelo Bowties	www.dangelobowties.com/
Designer Heaven	www.designerheaven.com/
Dickies	www.dickies.com/
Digities Neckwear	www.digities.com/

Dressed by Scotland	www.dressedbyscotland.co.uk/
Duckhead Apparel Online Store	www.duckhead.com/
Eddie Bauer	www.eddiebauer.com/
Edward Teach	www.edward-teach.com/
Elephant and Castle	www.elephantandcastle.com.au/
Embleton & King	www.embletonking.com/
eSuit.com	www.esuit.com/
Ex Officio	www.exofficio.com/
Execstyle	www.execstyle.com/
Fabric8	www.fabric8.com/
Factory Direct Menswear	www.factorydirectmenswear.com/
FASHIonLINE	www.fashionline.co.at/
Fashion Man	www.fashionman.com/
Fat Face Online Store	www.fatface.co.uk/
Fiducia Collection	www.fiduciacollection.com/
Flyz	www.flyz.net/
Fruit of the Loom	www.fruit.com/
Galleria Mall Online	www.galleriamallonline.com/
Gentlemen's Essentials	www.gentlemensessentials.com/
G.H. Bass & Co.	www.ghbass.com/
Gramicci	www.gramicci.com/
Haburi.com	www.haburi.com/
Hackett	www.hackett.co.uk/
Hampton Point	www.hamptonpoint.com/
Harolds	www.harolds.com/

Hart Schaffner and Marx	www.hartschaffnermarx.com/
Harvie & Hudson	www.harvieandhudson.com/
Heralds	www.heraldsmenswear.com/
Herringbone	www.herringbone.com.au/
High and Mighty	www.highandmighty.co.uk/
Hilditch & Key	www.hilditch.co.uk/
Hucklecote Country Clothing	www.hucklecote.co.uk/
Hugestore.com	www.hugestore.com/
Hunters Tie Partnership	www.luxuryties.com/
Ike Behar	www.ikebehar.com/
International Jock	internationaljock.com/
Island Shirts	islandshirts.com/
Jcrew.com	www.jcrew.com/catalog/
J. David's Custom Clothiers	www.jdavids.com/
Jeffrey's Collections	www.jeffreyscollections.com/
Kelsey Tailors	www.kelseytailors.co.uk/
Kingsize clothes	www.kingsizeclothes.co.uk/
Kiniki	www.kiniki.com/
Loose Cannon Apparel Ltd	www.loosecannon.net/
M. Goldberg Clothier	www.mgoldbergclothier.com/
Makola African Fashion Boutique	www.makolaboutique.com/
Male Manor	www.malemanor.com/
Maus and Hoffman	mausandhoffman.com/
Men's Clothes on Sale	www.eddiebauer.com/
Men's Clothing	www.smartcasual.com/

Milbern Clothing	www.milbern.com/
Milepost Four	www.milepostfour.com/
Moonbow Tropics Maui	moonbowtropicsmaui.com/
Muldoon's Men's Clothing	www.muldoons.com/
Necktie Organizer	www.necktieorganizer.com/
Neckwear Directory	www.neckweardirectory.com/
Niftythreads.com	www.niftythreads.com/
Novelty Ties by Uniquely Tied	www.noveltyneckties.com/
Ocean Pacific Canada	www.op.ca/
Oldnavy.com	www.oldnavy.com/
OneHanesPlace	www.onehanesplace.com/
Paradise Apparel	www.paradiseapparel.com/
Paul Fredrick	www.paulfredrick.com/
Pendleton Woolen Mills	www.pendleton-usa.com/
Peter Magee	www.pmshirts.com/
PFI - America's Western Store	www.pfiwestern.com/
Portal Jack	www.portaljack.com/
Principles	www.principles.co.uk/
Rage Against Retail	www.rageagainstretail.com/
Renton Western Wear	www.rentonww.com/
Rolli-Moden	www.rolli-moden.com/
Rym Stuff	www.rymstuff.com/
S and K Menswear	www.skmenswear.com/
Sansabelt Pant World	sansabeltworld.com/
SaviShopper	www.savishopper.com/

Sax Design	**www.saxdesign.com/**
Sergeant's Western World	**www.sergeantswestern.com/**
Seymour Shirts	**www.seymour-shirts.co.uk/**
Shacker.com	**www.shacker.com/**
Shirt Press	**www.shirt-press.co.uk/**
Shop Fords	**shopfords.com/**
Silk Shop London	**www.silkshoplondon.com/**
Skivvy	**www.skivvy.com/**
Slates	**www.slates.com/**
Sportique International	**www.sportiqueinternational.com/**

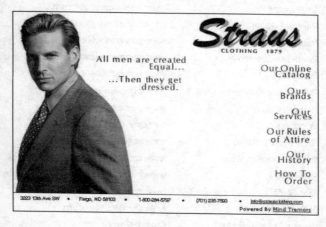

Straus Clothing	**strausclothing.com/**
Suitable	**www.suitable-u.com/**

Suitbank.com	www.suitbank.com/
Syms Clothing	www.syms.com/index.html
Tabasco Ties	www.tabascogolfshirts.com/
Territory Ahead	www.territoryahead.com/
Tie Saver	www.tiesaver.co.uk/
Tieguys.com	www.tieguys.com/
Tiemaster	www.tiemaster.com/
Ties 4 all	www.ties4all.co.uk/
Ties Factory	www.the-ties-factory.com/
Tieshop UK	www.tieshop.uk.com/
TiesTiesNeckties.com	www.tiestiesneckties.com/
Tom James	www.tomjamesco.com/
Tommy Hilfiger	www.tommy.com/
Top Drawers	www.topdrawers.com/
Top Man	www.topman.co.uk/
Uglies Boxer Shorts	www.uglies.com/
Ultimate Outlet – Fashion	www.ultimateoutlet.com/shop/fashion_main.asp
Ventresca	www.ventresca.com/
Walking Man	www.walkingman.com/
WebUndies	www.webundies.com/
WildTies.com	www.wildties.com/
Wm Fox	www.wmfox.com/
World-Ties.com	www.world-ties.com/
Youngor Group	www.youngorgroup.com/
Yourunderwear.com	www.yourunderwear.com/

Children's Clothes

Children grow so fast that they need plenty of clothes but it's often difficult to get the correct size. Many of these clothes stores offer sizing advice.

ABC Global Shopper	www.abcglobalshopper.com/kids
Alex and Me Solar Protection	www.alexandme.com/
Amber Rose Fleece	www.amberrosefleece.com/
Anichini	www.anichini.net/
Annex Shoppe	www.annexshoppe.com/
Ara's Pants	www.araspants.com/
Beebop Inc.com	www.beebopinc.com/
Best Dressed Kids	www.bestdressedkids.com/
Bombalulus	www.bombalulus.com/
BoomersKids	www.boomerskids.com/
Brandoni-USA	www.brandoni-usa.com/
Breyla Children's Clothing	www.breyla.com/
Bubby Wear Australia	www.bubby.com.au/
Carol Holm Design	www.holmdesign.com/
Charlie Crow Dressing up	www.charliecrow.com/
Childrens Closet	www.thechildrenscloset.com/
Children's Clothes Exchange	www.textilefiberspace.com/a/tx6030.html
Children's Place	www.childrensplace.com/
Chloe's Designs	www.chloesdesigns.com/
Classy Kids	www.classykids.com/

Clothes Closet	clothescloset.netfirms.com/
Clothing Exchange	childrentoday.com/resources/articles/clothes.htm
CO2 Girl	www.co2girl.com/
Connie's Kids	www.connieskids.com/
Cookie Crumbs!	www.go.to/cookiecrumbs
Cotton Moon	www.cottonmoon.co.uk/
Country Lane Kids	www.countrylanekids.com/
Crocodile Tears	www.crocodiletears.com.au/
Crumbsnatchers	www.crumbsnatchers.net/
Cute Children's Clothes Co	www.cutechildrensclothes.com/
DapperLads	www.dapperlads.com/
Debbie Bliss Knitwear	www.debbiebliss.freeserve.co.uk/
Delaware Children's Clothing	www.beach-net.com/shopclotheskidsdel.html
Designs by Augusta	www.designsbyaugusta.com/
Dragonfly Children's Clothes	www.dragonflys.co.uk/
Echo Field Cottons	www.echofield.com/
Emily Kate's	www.emilykates.com/
Emma T. Clothing	www.emmat.com/
Emmala Children's Clothing	www.emmala.com/
Euro 4 Kids	www.euro4kids.com/
Exciting Inc	www.excitinginc.com/
Exclusively Jenny	www.exclusivelyjenny.com/
First Squad	www.militarybratwear.com/
Fleece Farm	www.fleecefarm.com/

Flora and Henri	www.florahenri.com/
French Kids	www.frenchkids.com/
Frog N' Princess	frogandprincess.anthill.com/
Gap Kids.com	www.gap.com/onlinestore/ gapkids/
Gatefish.com	www.gatefish.com/
Golden Giraffe	www.goldengiraffe.com/
Guppy Gear	www.guppy-gear.com/
Hanna Andersson Clothing	www.hannaandersson.com/
Hanna'La	www.hannala.com/
Heather's Children's Clothing	www.heathersclothing.com/
HipHemp!	www.hiphemp.com/
Hopscotch Dressing Up Clothes	www.hopscotchmailorder.co.uk/
Infant Replays	www.infantreplays.com/
InStyle Kids	www.instylekids.com/
Iris's of Penzance	www.66penzance.fsnet.co.uk/
Isabel Garreton Inc.	www.isabelgarreton.com/
Jakpot Outlet shopping mall	members.tripod.com/~jakpot/ index1.html
Just 4 Kix	www.just4kix.com/
Just Kids Clothes	www.justkidsclothes.com/
K4	www.k4web.com/kidsclothes
Kid Canada Clothing	www.kidcanadaclothing.com/
Kid Knits	www.island.net/~rjbw/ kidknits.html

Kid Style-nyc	www.kidstyle-nyc.com/
Kids' Clothes	www.urchin.co.uk/
Kids' Clothes	www.thefamilystore.com/
Kids + Clothes	www.stretcher.com/stories/ 990920g.cfm
Kids' Clothesline	www.kidscl.com/
Kids' Clothing	www.storks-store.com/ clothes4kids
Kids' Fashion Center	www.webmall2000.net/fashion/
Kids' Fashion Online	www.sewingmall.com/fashion/ kids.htm
Kids' T-shirts	www.kids-t-shirt.com/
Kids' Used Clothes	kidsclothingsale.home.mindspring .com/
kids4clothes	www.kids4clothes.i12.com/
Kidstock	www.kidstockmontana.com/
Kidswear Directory	www.kidsweardirectory.com/
Kidz Cargo	www.kidzcargo.com/
King's Kidz Infant Apparel	www.kingskidz.com/
Kings and Sages Apparel	www.kingsandsages.com/
Lauren Alexandra	www.laurenalexandra.com/
Lil' Cuties Boutique	www.lilcutiesboutique.com/
Little Boutique	www.littleboutique.com/
Little Red Coat Co	www.littleredcoat.com/
Littleapple	www.littleapple.com.ar/
Lolly's Tot Shop	www.lollystotshop.com/

Lucy Jayne Collection	www.lucy-jayne.co.uk/
Mad River Clothing	www.madriverclothing.com/
Marese	www.marese.co.uk/
Masque Rays	www.sunproof.com/children2000.htm
Material Girl Fashions	www.materialgirlfashions.com/
Max and Ruby	maxandruby.com/
Mischief	www.mischiefkids.co.uk/
MommyDana Sales	www.mommydana.com/
Nameosaurus	www.nameosaurus.com/
Nana's Kids Kloset	www.nanaskidskloset.com/
Nowa Li	www.nowali.com/
Oilily	www.oililyusa.com/
Okjas Kids	www.k4web.com/kidsclothes
One of a Kind Kid	www.oneofakindkid.com/
Orient Expressed	www.orientexpressed.com/catalog/homepage.html
Originali-tees	www.originali-tees.com/
OshKosh B'Gosh	www.oshkoshbgosh.com/
Over The Moon Babywear	www.overthemoon-babywear.co.uk/
Pageant Shoppe	www.thepageantshoppe.com/
Patricia Smith	www.patriciasmith.co.uk/
Petit Patapon	www.petitpatapon.com/
Pip-Squeeks	www.pip-squeeks.com/
Precious Child	www.precious-child.com/

Precious Little Time	www.preciouslittletime.com/
Pride and Joy	www.pridejoy.org/
Ptarmigan Kids	www.ptarmigankids.com/
Punkey Monkey	www.punkeymonkey.com/
Ragamuffins	www.ragamuffins-children.com/
RAJ Shop	www.rajinc.com/
Rich Kids	www.rich-kids.com/
Robyn Boyd	www.robynboyd.com.au/
Sara's Prints	www.sarasprints.com/
SeaWeeds	www.kvproducts.com/SeaWeeds/
Shoe Zoo	www.shoezoo-mpls.com/
Spiff Clothing Company	www3.bc.sympatico.ca/spiff
Splashcity	www.splashcity.com/kids.htm
Spoilt Rotten	www.onthenet.com.au/~wild
Sprouts Clothes 4 Kids	www.clothes4kids.com/
Storybook Heirlooms	www.storybookheirlooms.com/
Taylor Rose	www.taylorrose.com/
Tessakids.com	www.tessakids.com/
That's My Boy	www.thatsmyboy.com/
TinyBlessings.com	www.tinyblessings.com/
Tody Bullmoose	www.todybullmoose.com/
Tot Towels	www.tottowels.com/
Trotters	www.trotters.co.uk/
WebClothes.com	www.webclothes.com/children childrens_clothing.htm
Weebok.com	www.weebok.com/

Baby Clothes

Before they get to the 'children' stage, you'll need plenty of baby clothes.

A Anichini	www.anichini.net/
A Special Day	www.a-special-day.com/
A Weefurbished Womb	www.weefurbished.com/
Alexis USA	www.alexisusa.com/
Anna-Bean Clothing Inc	www.annabean.com/
Annette's CraftWorld	home.ican.net/~acraftwd
ASAP Manufacturing	www.asapmfg.com/
Aunt Hilda's Baby Clothes	members.tripod.com/~aunthilda/
Babblin' Babies	www.babblinbabies.com/
Baby Armadillo Clothing	www.albany.net/~smiles/
Baby Amore	www.babyamore.com/
Baby Bee Hat Company	www.babybeehats.com/
Baby Blessing Outfits	whatablessing.bizland.com/
Baby Blessings	www.babyblessings.com/
Baby Campus.com	www.babycampus.com/clothes
Baby Catalogue	www.thebabycatalogue.com/
Baby Clothing Online	babyclothingonline.com/
Baby Fish Blues	babyfishblues.com/
Baby Gap	www.gap.com/onlinestore/babygap/
Baby Hats	babyhats.homestead.com/
Baby Nouveau	www.babynouveau.com/

Baby Style	www.babystyle.com/
Baby Ultimate	www.babyultimate.com/
Baby World	www.binary.co.nz/babyw.html
Babybows	www.babybows.com/
Babyjay layette	www.babyjay.com/
Babyrobes.com	www.babyrobes.com/
Bareware	www.bareware.net/
Bearskins Baby Wear	www.bearskins.com.au/
Bergstroms Childrens Stores	www.bergstroms.com/
Biz Nest	www.biznest.com/babies/
Bobux USA	www.bobuxusa.net/
Body By Prayer	www.bodybyprayer.com/
Breyla	www.bcity.com/breyla
Buy For Kids	www.buyforkids.com/
Caleb's Corner	www.calebscorner.com/
Cheekaboo	www.cheekaboo.com/
Childrenswear.com	www.childrenswear.com/
Chock Catalog Baby Store	www.chockcatalog.com/
Christening Boutique	christeningboutique.com/
Coccole	www.expoumbria.com/coccole
Cookie Baby Inc.	www.cookiebabyinc.com/
Cute As A Bug	www.cuteasabug.com/
Dyed in Vermont	tie-dyes.com/
Earth Muffinzz Baby Clothes	www.earthmuffinzz.com/
Earthwear Cotton Originals	www.earth-wear.com/

Eco baby	www.ecobaby.ie/
Eva Evan	www.evaevan.com/
Exciting Inc.	excitinginc.com/
Exclusively Jenny	www.exclusivelyjenny.com/
EZ-Baby	www.ez-baby.com/
First Step	www.bestforbabies.com/
GahGah.com	www.gahgah.com/
Good Lad	www.goodlad.com/
Google Designs	www.googledesigns.com/
Green Babies	www.greenbabies.com/
Hanna Andersson	www.hannaandersson.com/
Hats by Sarah	www.albabe.com/hatsbysarah/
Hi Baby!	www.hibaby.com/
Hindsight Diapers by Jennifer	www.hindsightdiapers.findhere.com/
James Collier Creations	www.jamescolliercreations.cc/
Jan's Knits For Kids	www.jansknitsforkids.com/
JoJo Maman Bebe	www.jojomamanbebe.co.uk/
Julie's Stuff	www.juliesstuff.com/
Katydids Christening Gowns	www.katydids.net/
Kieraninc.com	www.kieraninc.com/
Layette Express	www.giftforbaby.net/
Le Petite Baby	no-odor.com/preemie/
Linda Manley	handmade.iocus.com/
Little Lids	www.littlelids.com/
Little Me	www.littleme.com/

Little Miracles Clothes	www.christeningbaby.com/
Little Prince and Princess	www.royalbaby.com/
Little Tapiocas	www.littletapiocas.com/
Lolly's Tot Shop	www.lollystotshop.com/
Made by Josette	www.eeguide.com/shops/josette/
Millennium Baby	www.millenniumbaby.com/
Miller-Dexter Christening Gowns	www.miller-dexter.com/
Moonjumpers	www.moonjumpers.com/
Mothercare	www.mothercare.com/
Mushroom House Designs	www.mushroomhousedesigns.com/
My Feherchild	www.angelfire.com/fl2/feherchild/
My Little Miracle	mars.superlink.net/mikebell
mySimon	www.mysimon.com/
Names In Knit	www.namesinknit.com/
Nap Sack Inc.	napsack-frenchimports.com/
Neonatal Support Group	www.neonatalsupport.co.uk/
Oliebollen.com	www.oliebollen.com/ob210_clothes.asp
Only Young Once	www.babyclothers.com/
Over The Moon Babywear	www.overthemoon-babywear.co.uk/
Peekaboocanada	www.peekaboocanada.com/
Polar Babies Clothing	www.polarbabies.com/
Poppy Childrenswear	www.poppy-children.co.uk/

Preemie Clothes	www.preemiesleepers.com/
Preemies Only	www.preemiesonly.com/
Roaming Wild!	www.roamingwild.com/
Snug As A Bug	www.snugasabug.com/
Snugglewrap	www.snugglewrap.com/
Spunky Punk	www.spunkypunk.com/
Stellina Baby Clothes	www.stellina.com/
Swim Diapers	www.gabbys.net/
Tesco – Baby and Toddler Store	www.tesco.com/babystore/
Tiny Little Clothes. Inc	www.tinylittleclothes.com/
Tiny Treasures Baby Clothes	www.baby-clothes-store.com/
Tizzyfits	www.tizzyfits.com/
Tootaloo	tootaloo.com/
Urchin	www.urchin.co.uk/
Vaco's	www.vaco.be/
Warm Beginnings by Danielle	www.warmbeginnings.com/
Wavin' Baby Designs	www.wavinbaby.com/
Wee Shop	www.weeshop.com/
Wish Upon A Star	www.wishkids.com/

Maternity Wear

Even earlier, is the maternity stage when it's the mum-to-be that needs lots of new clothes.

| 9 Months Plus | www.9monthsplus.com/ |
| Abracadabra Maternity | www.momshop.com/ |

Anna Cris Maternity	www.annacris.com/
Baby Becoming	www.babybecoming.com/
BabyZone's Maternity Zone	www.maternityzone.com/
Basics Direct	www.maternity.com/
BeBeMaternity	www.bebematernity.com/
Bellemere	www.bellemere.com/
Belly Belt	www.cyberbaby.com.au/bellybelt
BellyBand	www.campusdirectory.com/bellyband/
Bloom'n Fashion	www.bloom-n.com/
Blooming Marvellous	www.bloomingmarvellous.co.uk/
Bumpstart	www.bumpstart.co.uk/
Carla C. Maternitywear	www.carla-c.com/
Clark and Lou Inc	www.bellybra.com/
Designer Maternity Clothing	www.professionalmaternity.com/
Details Direct	www.detailsdirect.com/pregkit.htm
eMommie.com	www.emommie.com/
Essential Baby	www.essentialbaby.com.au/
Expecting Style	www.expectingstyle.com/
Fit Maternity and Beyond	www.fitmaternity.com/
From Here to Maternity	www.fromheretomaternity.com/
Generations Maternity	www.gmaternity.com/
Gladstone Maternity Outlet	www.momstobe.com/
Healthy Legs and Feet Too	maternitystockings.com/
Hindy's	www.maternityapparel.com/

iMaternity.com	www.imaternity.com/
Jake & Me Clothing Company	www.jakeandme.com/
Kyra Mommy Wear	www.kyrawear.com/
Ladies in Waiting Maternity	ladiesinwaitingmaternity.com/
Mama Bella	www.mamabella.com/
Mama T's Nursing Wear	www.mama-ts.com/
Maternal Instinct	www.maternal-instinct.com/
Maternity and Beyond	www.maternityandbeyond.com/
Maternity and Preemie	www.akmaternity.com/
Maternity Blues	www.mbbmarketing.com/
Maternity by Veronique	www.veroniqued.com/
Maternity Closet	www.maternitycloset.com/
Maternity Clothing with Style	www.stylematernity.com/
Maternity Directory	www.maternitydirectory.com/
Maternity For Less	maternity4less.com/
Maternity Outfitters Inc	www.maternityoutfitters.com/
Maternity Profile	www.maternityprofile.com/
Maternity Stop	www.maternitystop.com/
Mom & Me Maternity	www.momandmematernity.com/
Mom and Me	www.mom-and-me.com/
Mom's to Be	www.momstobefashions.com/ prod01.htm
Mom's Tops	users.ev1.net/~momstops/ default.htm
Moms to Be Factory Outlet	www.momstobefashions.com/
Moms Trends	www.momstrends.com/

Monterrosa Embroidery	www.monterrosa.com/
Motherhood Maternity	www.motherhood.com/
Mothers In Motion Inc.	www.mothers-in-motion.com/
Mothers' Online Thrift Shop	www.motshop.com/
Mumsies	www.mumsies.com/
Naissance	naissancematernity.com/
Ninemonths-etc.com	www.ninemonths-etc.com/
One Hot Mama	www.onehotmama.com/
Pamper Mum	www.pampermum.com.au/
Pea in the Pod	www.apeainthepod.com/
Pickles and Ice Cream	www.plusmaternity.com/
Professional Expectations	www.maternityleasing.com/
Save-A-Bundle	www.save-a-bundle.com/
theMaternityShop.com	www.thematernityshop.com/
Thyme Maternity	www.maternity.ca/
Two in One Maternity Wear	www.twoinone.com.au/
Village Belle	www.villagebelle.com/
With Child	www.withchild.com/

Shoes

If you do buy from an online shoe-shop, check the postal charges carefully because shoes are heavy and so delivery can be expensive. Also make sure the online store offers an exchange if the shoes don't fit properly.

123Shoes.com	www.123shoes.com/

800shoes.com	**800shoes.com/**
A Step Above	**www.astepaboveshoes.com/**
A Step Apart	**shoes-comfort-fashion.com/**
Alan's Shoes	**www.shoes.com/**
Allen Edmonds	**www.allenedmonds.com/**
Altama	**www.altama.com/tactical.html**
Antshoes	**www.antshoes.com.au/**
Aquila Shoes	**www.aquila.com.au/**
Arcopedico Shoes	**www.arcopedicoshoes.com/**
Atelier Fusaro Shoes	**www.fusaro.de/**
Aurora Shoes	**www.aurorashoes.com/**
Barrington Outfitters	**gbshoes.com/**
Bay Street Shoes	**www.baystreetshoes.com/**
Best Shoes	**www.thebestshoes.com/**
BN Safety Footwear	**www.bnsafetyfootwear.com/**
BootBarn.com	**www.bootbarn.com/**
Boots Online	**www.bootsonline.com.au/**
Breyer International	**www.breyerintl.com/**
Brown Shoes	**www.brown-shoes.com/**
Butcher and Company	**www.butcherco.com/**
Capps Shoe Company	**www.capps-shoe.com/**
Celtic Sheepskin Company	**www.celtic-sheepskin.co.uk/**
Chester Boot Shop	**www.chesterboot.com/**
Chet's Shoes	**www.chetsshoes.com/**
Clobber Leather	**www.clobberleather.com.au/**

Clog and Shoe Workshop	www.clogandshoe.co.uk/
Clog Shoppe	www.theclogshoppe.com/
Clog Store	theclogstore.com/
Clogs-N-More	www.clogsnmore.com/
Clogworld	www.clogworld.com/
Cloudwalkers	www.cloudwalkers.com/
Correct Shoe Fitters	www.correctshoefitters.com/
Crary Shoes	www.craryshoes.com/
Crummies	www.handcraftedshoes.com/
Cudas	www.cudas.com/
Dale's Shoes	www.dales-shoes.com/
Dansko Inc	www.dansko.com/
Davidson Shoes Plus	www.shoestoboot.com/
Dee Shoes	deeshoes.com/
Deer Stags Shoes	www.deerstags.com/
Di Bucci Shoes	www.dbshoes.com/
Dinoia Shoes	www.italianshoestore.com/
Dunham Boots	dunhamboots.com/
Espadrilles	espadrillesetc.com/
Ethical Wares	www.veganvillage.co.uk/ ethicalwares/
Factory Shoe Outlet	www.factoryshoeoutlet.com/
Fantastique Shoes	www.npnhost.com/footwear
Fitted Shoe	www.fittedshoe.com/
Foot Smart	www.footsmart.com/

Footwear Directory	www.footweardirectory.com/
Frumps	www.frumps.com/
Gravis Footwear	www.gravisfootwear.com/
Great Lakes Shoe Company	www.mephistogreatlakes.com/
Great Plains Moccasin Factory	www.uvisions.com/moccasin
Grenda Shoe Corporation	www.grendha.com/
Guat Shoes	www.guatshoes.co.uk/
Happy Feet	www.happyfeet.com/
Hard Time Boots	www.hardtimeboots.com/
Howards Shoes	www.howardsshoes.com/
Hush Puppies Shoes	hushpuppiesshoes.com/
Inge's Footwear	www.ingesfootwear.com/
Ippy Clog and Sandal Company	www.shore.net/~mia/
J.W. Bray Slippers	www.jwbray.com/
Jgear	www.jgearusa.com/
Joewear	www.joewear.com/
Just Our Shoes	www.justourshoes.com/
K and L Boots	www.kandlboots.com/
Kaibab Moccasins	www.kaibabmocs.com/
Key West Sandal Factory	www.kwsf.com/
Lavahut	www.lavahut.com/feet.htm
Leatherlife Sheepskins	www.uggboots.ws/
Lee's Shopping Mall	www.leesonline.com/index.html
Les Newmans	www.lesnewmans.com/
Lonnie's Ballroom	www.lonniesdance.com/

Louie	www.netlouie.com/
Marley of London	www.marleylondon.com/
Meredith Trading Post	www.meredithtradingpost.com/
Michele Olivieri	moshoes.com/
Mischief	www.mischiefkids.co.uk/footwear.html
Moccasin Shop	www.mocshop.com/
MyFavoriteShoe.com	www.myfavoriteshoe.com/
New England Shoe Outlet	newenglandshoe.com/
New Balance	www.newbalancestlouis.com/
Nicole Shoes	www.nicoleshoes.com/
Online Shoes	www.onlineshoes.com/
Pedestrian Shops	www.comfortableshoes.com/
Pennies On The Dollar.com	www.shoes-discount-shoes.com/
Perfect Sandal	www.aperfectsandal.com/
Platform Shoes	shop4shoes.com/
Posh Footwear	www.eclogs.com/
RainCity Footwear	www.raincityfootwear.com/
Rapid Shoe Store	www.bootrepair.com/
Red Wing Shoes	rwss.com/
ReSole Center	www.resolectr.com/
Reyers	www.reyers.com/
Reynolds Shoes	www.shoes.com.nf/
Rock River	www.rockriver.com/
Rockport Shoes	www.walking-shoes.com/

Rocky Shoes and Boots Inc.	**www.rockyboots.com/**
Rogan's Shoes	**www.rogansshoes.com/**
Rousabout	**rous-uggs.com/**
Sandalz	**www.sandalz.com/**
Sebago.com	**www.sebago.com/**
Sha Sha	**www.sha-sha.com/**
Shandra Fashions	**www.shandrafashions.com/ shoes.htm**
Shipton and Heneage Ltd	**www.shiphen.com/**
Shoe Dept.	**www.shoedept.com/**
Shoe Parlor	**www.shoeparlor.com/**
Shoe Superstore	**www.shoesuperstore.com/**
Shoe Town	**www.sbshoetown.com/**
Shoebuy.com	**www.shoebuy.com/**
Shoecomfort.com	**www.shoecomfort.com/**
Shoemadness	**www.shoemadness.com/**
Shoepad	**www.shoepad.com/**
Shoes of The Fisherman	**www.shoesofthefisherman.com/**
Shoes On The Net	**www.shoesonthenet.com/**
Shoe-Shack.com	**www.shoe-shack.com/**
Shoo Be Doo	**www.shoobedoo.com/**
Shop Outerwear.com	**www.shopouterwear.com/**
Siam Leather Goods	**www.siamleathergoods.com/**
Simple Shoes	**www.rack-pack.com/**
Simply Australian	**www.simplyoz.com/**

Skechers Inc	www.skechers.com/
Slogger's Footwear	www.sloggers.com/
Sof Sole	www.sofsole.com/
Soho Shoe Salon	www.sohoshoe.com/
Sole Survivor	leathersandals.com/
Stacy Adams Men's Shoes	www.stacyadams.com/
Steger Mukluks and Moccasins	www.mukluks.com/
Stegmann	clogz.com/
Stravers	www.stravers-adam.demon.nl/
Studio HD2 Shoes	www.studio-hd2.com/

Sunrise Shoes	www.sunriseshoes.net/
Sunsports Sandal	www.sunhemp.com/
Supreme Comfort Footwear	www.workboots.org/
Tanner's Cobbler Shop	www.tanners-cobbler.com/
Teva Sport Sandals	www.tevasandals.com/
Timberline Outfitters	www.tlpg.com/
Tokio Kumagaï	www.tokiok.com/
Tony Shoes Inc.	www.tonyshoes.com/
Tony's Shoe Store	www.shoestoreusa.com/
Tozzok	www.tozzok.com/
Tradition World	www.traditionworld.com/
Vegetarian Shoes	www.vegetarian-shoes.co.uk/

| Via Moda | **www.viamoda.com/** |
| Via Veneto Shoes | **viavenetoshoes.com/** |

Walk Shop	**walkshop.com/**
Walking Company	**www.walkingco.com/**
Walking on Water	**www.walkingonwater.com/**
Wicked Road Warrior	**www.wickedroadwarrior.com/**
Worksite Footwear	**www.worksitefootwear.com/**
Zappos.com	**www.zappos.com/**

Computers

If you've got a computer, the Internet is a great place to make it better by installing more software or adding to the hardware.

Hardware

Not only complete computer systems, but components are available to buy on the web. Most companies also provide technical specifications of their products and many provide free drivers for their hardware.

3Com	**www.3com.com/**
Adaptec	**www.adaptec.com/**
AMD	**www.amd.com/**
Apple Computer, Inc.	**www.apple.com/**
ATI Technologies	**www.atitech.ca/**
Cirrus Logic	**www.cirrus.com/**
Cisco	**www.cisco.com/**
Cyrix	**www.cyrix.com/**
Dabs	**www.dabs.com/**
Dell Computers	**www.dell.com/**

Discounts Online   www.discounts.co.nz/

Fujitsu	www.fujitsu.com/
G²	www.gsquared.net/
Games Terminal	www.gamesterminal.com/
Gateway	www.gateway.com/
Hayes Corporation	www.hayes.com/
Hewlett-Packard	www.hp.com/
Hitachi	www.hitachi.com/
IBM Corporation	www.ibm.com/
Intel Corporation	www.intel.com/
Iomega	www.iomega.com/
Jungle	www.jungle.com/
Micro Warehouse	www.microwarehouse.co.uk/
Micrologic	www.micro-logic.com/
Modern Computers	www.moderncomputers.com/
Motorola	www.mot.com/
NEC Online	www.nec.com/

NVIDIA	www.nvidia.com/
OPTi	www.opti.com/
PC World	www.pcworld.co.uk/
PC2GO	www.pc2go.co.uk/
Philips	www.philips.com/
Planet Micro	www.planetmicro.co.uk/
Quantum	www.quantum.com/
Rockwell	www.rockwell.com/
Samsung	www.samsung.com/
Seagate	www.seagate.com/
Simply Computers	www.simply.co.uk/
Sony	www.sony.com/
Sun Microsystems	www.sun.com/
SyQuest	www.syquest.com/
Tiny Computers	www.tiny.com/
Toshiba	www.toshiba.com/

U.S. Robotics	www.usr.com/
Unisys	www.unisys.com/
Western Digital Corporation	www.wdc.com/

| Xircom | www.xircom.com/ |
| Zilog Inc. | www.zilog.com/ |

Computer Consumables

A car needs petrol, a house needs electricity and a computer requires paper and ink.

Action	www.action.com/
Lindy	www.lindy.com/
Misco	www.misco.co.uk/
Viking	www.vikingdirect.com/
Vista Papers	www.vistapapers.co.uk/

Software

There are countless Internet sites that offer software which can be downloaded either for free or for a nominal sum.

Download Shop	www.downloadshop.co.uk/
Download.com	www.download.com/
Downloads at MSN	msn.co.uk/Page/4-30.asp
EuroNet – TUCOWS	tucows.euro.net/
Free Stuff Link Center	centerfree.hypermart.net/
FreeSoft97 Freeware	www.freesoft97.mcmail.com/
Grey Olltwit's Freeware	www.adders.org/freeware/
Linux Software Archive	linux.davecentral.com/

Microsoft Download Center	www.microsoft.com/downloads/search.asp
Netscape	www.netscape.com/
Rocketdownload.com	www.rocketdownload.com/
TUCOWS	tucows.ukonline.co.uk/
UK Games	www1.zdnet.com/cgwuk/
VNU	www.vnunet.com/download
WinFiles.com	www.winfiles.com/
WinZip Download Page	www.winzip.com/download.htm
ZDNet Software	www.zdnet.co.uk/software/

Games

The vast majority of downloadable programs are games for PCs. Some of these sites also deal in games for consoles like Sega, Nintendo and Playstation.

24 Hour Games	www.free-gaming.com/
3D Gamers	www.3dgamers.com/
All Games Network	www.allgames.com/
ASC Games	www.ascgames.com/
Bungie	www.bungie.org/
Can't Beat It? Cheat It!	www.cheatit.com/previews.htm
Computer Games at Planet Click	www.planetclick.com/
Computer Games Online	www.cdmag.com/
ComputerGameFan	www.compufan.com/
CrazyGames	www.crazygames.net/

DaGameBoyz	www.dagameboyz.com/
Daily Telefrag	www.dailytelefrag.com/
DOS Games Page	www.dosgames.com/
Eidos Interactive	www.eidosinteractive.com/
ESPN Fantasy Games	games.espn.go.com/
Extacy Games	www.extacygames.com/
Free Games Net	www.free-games-net.com/
FreeGames	freegames.org/
Funster Multiplayer Word Games	www.funster.com/
Game Addict	www.gameaddict.net/
Game Forge	www.game-forge.com/
Game Nexus	www.gamenexus.com/
Game Search	www.gamesearch.co.uk/
Game Stats	www.gamestats.com/
GameArchives	www.gamearchives.com/
GameArena	www.gamearena.net/
Gamer's Depot	www.gamersdepot.com/main.htm
Gamers Homepage	gamershomepage.com/
Gamers' CyberMall	gcm.hypermart.net/
Gamersnews	www.gamersnews.com/
GamerXtreme	www.gamerxtreme.com/
Games and Videos	www.gamesandvideos.com/
Games Domain	www.gamesdomain.co.uk/
Games Express	www.gamesexpress.net/
Games (Microsoft) UK	www.microsoft.com/uk/games/

Games Paradise	www.gamesparadise.com/hme/hmepge.asp
GameSpot UK	www.gamespot.co.uk/
GamesZone	www.gameszone.co.uk/
Gamez Unlimited	www.gamezunlimited.com/
Gamezilla!	www.gamezilla.com/
GamezNet	www.gameznet.com/3dgames
GameZone.com	www.gamezone.com/
Hotgames	www.hotgames.com/
IGN PC	pc.ign.com/
Jungle.com	www.jungle.com/play/
LadyDragon.Com	www.ladydragon.com/
LucasArts	www.lucasarts.com/
Media and Games Online	www.mgon.com/
MobyGames	www.mobygames.com/
OnTracks	www.ontracks.co.uk/
PC Game.com	www.pcgame.com/
PC Game Review	www.pcgr.com/
PC Game Watch	www.pcgamewatch.com/
PC Gamer Online	www.pcgamer.co.uk/
PC Gamers	www.pcgamers.net/
PC Gameworld	www.pcgameworld.com/buygames.htm
Productive Play Company	www.prodplay.co.uk/
Review Nexus	www.reviewnexus.com/
Riddler	www.riddler.com/

Soleau Software   www.soleau.com/
Sports Illustrated For Kids Games www.sikids.com/games/
                                    index2.html

Stomped   www.stomped.com/
Studio Magique   www.magique.com/
We Come To Play.com   www.wecometoplay.com/

Internet Search

If you want to find a particular piece of information, or you want
to find a site that will provide you with the information you need,
you could try a search engine. The trouble is that when you enter
your query into a search engine, you invariably get either nothing,

or 10,000 websites to wade through. It's for this reason that this guide is so popular.

All Search Engines	www.allsearchengines.co.uk/
AltaVista Search UK	www.altavista.co.uk/

Ask Jeeves (UK)	www.ask.co.uk/
Ask Jeeves (US)	www.askjeeves.com/
Excite United Kingdom	www.excite.co.uk/
FAST Search	www.alltheweb.com/
Google	google.com/
HotBot	www.hotbot.com/
Infoseek UK	www.infoseek.com/
LookSmart	www.looksmart.com/
Lycos	www.lycos.co.uk/
MSN Web Search	search.msn.co.uk/

Netscape Search	home.netscape.com/home/ internet-search.html
Northern Light	www.northernlight.com/
SearchUK	www.searchuk.com/

UK Plus	www.ukplus.co.uk/
WebCrawler	www.webcrawler.com/
Webseek	www.ctr.columbia.edu/webseek/
Yahoo	www.yahoo.com/

PC Help

Computer manuals are notoriously difficult to understand. If you get stuck, you could try one of these sites to help you get unstuck.

Booster	www.thirdage.com/features/tech/booster/
British Computer Society	www.bcs.org.uk/
Computer Home Help	www.almac.co.uk/homehelp/
ESupportLive	www.esupportlive.com/
HelpDesk.com	www.helpdesk.com/
MacUser OnLine	www.macuser.co.uk/
Microsoft Windows Update	windowsupdate.microsoft.com/
Newbies Guides	www.ug.cs.dal.ca/pub/newbie.html
PC Guide	www.pcguide.com/
PC Help	computers.iwz.com/beos/
PC Help Group	www.pchelp.net/
PC Help Online	www.pchelponline.com/
PC User Group - London	www.ibmpcug.co.uk/index.1html
Wanda's Web PC Help Center	www.wandaweb.com/pchelp/
ZDNet - Help and How-To	www.zdnet.com/zdhelp/

Web Design

Web pages are constructed using a language called HTML (HyperText Markup Language). You can buy programs which will help you create web pages without having to go into HTML, but it is still worth having some knowledge about it.

About HTML	**html.miningco.com/ compute/html/**
Bare Bones Guide to HTML	**werbach.com/barebones/ barebone.html**
Beginner's Guide to HTML	**burks.bton.ac.uk/burks/internet/ web/html_bg/html_bg.htm**
Beginning HTML	**htmlgoodies.earthweb.com/**
Enhanced HTML 2000	**www.enhance.co.uk/**
GettingStarted.net	**www.gettingstarted.net/**
Guide to HTML and CGI Scripts	**snowwhite.it.brighton.ac.uk/ ~mas/mas/courses/html/ html.html**
HTML Compendium	**www.htmlcompendium.org/**
HTML Help Homepage	**redrival.com/htmlgo/**
HTML Home Page	**www.w3.org/markup/**

Home | Contact | Advertise   DevStart.com Network

HTML Primer

—Navigate— Browse Search

HTML Primer	**htmlprimer.com/**
HTML Quick Reference	**www.cc.ukans.edu/~acs/docs/ other/HTML_quick.shtml**
HTML Quick Reference Guide	**www.ku.edu/acs/website.shtml**
Learn HTML in 7 Easy Steps	**html.digitalsea.net/**
Learn HTML Quick	**members.tripod.com/~MCTJDM/**

Nigel's HTML Tutorial

www.stonewall.demon.co.uk/
tutor/html/

Quick Guide to HTML

burks.bton.ac.uk/burks/internet/
web/quikhtml/qhtmltxt.htm

Animated GIFs

These are the little movies you see on webpages that make the page just a little more interesting.

Aardvark Animations Library

207.201.146.106/animations/

Animated GIFs

www.webdeveloper.com
animations/

Animation Factory

www.animfactory.com/

Clip Art Warehouse

www.clipart.co.uk/

Collection of Animated Gifs

www.geocities.com/SoHo/3505/
index.html

Custom Animations

web.islandnet.com/~luree/
animate/animate.html

Cybernettix Animated GIFs

www.cybernettix.vuurwerk.nl/
animated.html

Free Animated Graphics

www.animation-station.com/

GIF Animation on the WWW	**members.aol.com/royalef/ gifanim.htm**
GIF Construction Set	**www.mindworkshop.com/ alchemy/gifcon.html**
Making Animated GIFs	**www6.uniovi.es/gifanim/ gifmake.htm**
Movies, Etc	**pages.prodigy.com/coolie/ movies.htm**
Stepping Stones Animation	**www.ssanimation.com/ gallery.html**

Web Graphics	**www.njet.net/heikki**

Education

Learning is a lifelong activity and there's no shortage of ways to learn on the Internet.

Learning

These sites have superb educational content which, although aimed mainly at kids, adults will find enthralling.

BBC Education	www.bbc.co.uk/education/home/
Blackboard	www.blackboard.com/
bookacourse.com	www.bookacourse.com/
British Council	www.britishcouncil.org/education/
Campaign for Learning	www.campaign-for-learning.org.uk/home.htm
CH4 Schools	schools.channel4.com/
Department for Education and Skills	www.dfes.gov.uk/
Digital Education Network	www.edunet.com/
Education 4 Kids	www.edu4kids.com/

Education Home Page	www.eu.microsoft.com/uk/education/
Education Place	www.eduplace.com/
Education Unlimited	www.educationunlimited.co.uk/
Educational.com	www.educational.com/
Enchanted Learning	www.enchantedlearning.com/
Fun Factory	www.esw.co.uk/funfactory/
Funschool.com	www.funschool.com/
GCSE Revision	www.bbc.co.uk/education/revision
Gurlpages.com	www.gurlpages.com/
Int'l Centre for Distance Learning	www-icdl.open.ac.uk/
Kids.com	www.kidscom.com/
Learndirect	www.learndirect.co.uk/
Learning.com	www.learning.com/
Learning Materials	www.learning-materials.co.uk/
Linguaphone	www.linguaphone.co.uk/
London Grid for Learning	www.lgfl.net/
National Curriculum	www.nc.uk.net/
National Grid for Learning	www.ngfl.gov.uk/
Math.com	www.math.com/
Maths Games	atschool.eduweb.co.uk/ufa10/games.htm
Schools Net	www.schoolsnet.com/
Schools Online	sol.ultralab.anglia.ac.uk/pages/schools_online/

Sesame Street	www.ctw.org/
Studyweb	www.studyweb.com/
Thinkquest.org	www.thinkquest.org/
Top Marks	www.topmarks.co.uk/
Virtual Teaching Centre	vtc.ngfl.gov.uk/
Yahooligans	www.yahooligans.com/
Yuckiest Website	www.yucky.com/

Museums

It's difficult to know quite where to put this, but as they are all educational...

Andy Warhol Museum	www.warhol.org/
Archaeology at MSU	emuseum.mankato.msus.edu/
Beaulieu Car Museum	www.beaulieu.co.uk/
Black Country Museum	www.woden.com/dudley/museum.html
British Museum	www.british-museum.ac.uk/
Brooklands Museum	www.motor-software.co.uk/brooklands/
Butler Institute of American Art	www.butlerart.com/
Carnegie Museum of Art	www.clpgh.org/cma/
Cleveland Museum of Art	www.clemusart.com/
Contemporary Arts Museum of Houston	www.camh.org/
Crocker Art Museum	www.sacto.org/crocker/
Getty Information Institute	www.ahip.getty.edu/

Getty, J.Paul Museum   **www.getty.edu/museum/**

Hammond Museum   **www.hammondmuseum.org/**

Imperial War Museum   **www.iwm.org.uk/**

Ironbridge Gorge Museum   **www.ironbridge.org.uk/**

Jane Austen Museum   **www.janeaustenmuseum.org.uk/**

London Transport Museum   **www.ltmuseum.co.uk/**

Motorsports Hall of Fame   **www.mshf.com/**

Museum of Classical Archaeology **www.classics.cam.ac.uk/ark.html**

Museum of Contemporary Art   **www.mca.com.au/**

Museum of East Asian Art   **www.east-asian-art.co.uk/**

Museum of the History of Science **www.mhs.ox.ac.uk/**

MUSEUM OF LONDON

Welcome to the <u>Museum of London</u>, the largest, most comprehensive city museum in the world, telling the fascinating story of London from prehistoric times to the present day.

Museum of London   **www.museum-london.org.uk/**

Museum of the Moving Image   **www.bfi.org.uk/museum/**

Museum of Science	**www.mos.org/**
Museum of Science & Industry (UK)	**www.msim.org.uk/**
Museum of Science & Industry (US)	**www.msichicago.org/**
National Gallery of Art	**www.nga.gov/**
National Gallery of Australia	**www.nga.gov.au/**
National Gallery of Victoria	**www.ngv.vic.gov.au/**
National Maritime Museum	**www.nmm.ac.uk/**
National Museum of Photography, Film & Television	**www.nmpft.org.uk/**
National Museum of Scotland	**www.nms.ac.uk/**
National Portrait Gallery	**www.npg.si.edu/**
National Railroad Museum	**www.nationalrrmuseum.org/**
National Railway Museum	**www.nmsi.ac.uk/nrm/**
National Tramways Museum	**www.tramway.co.uk/about.html**
Natural History Museum	**www.nhm.ac.uk/**
Royal Air Force Museum	**www.rafmuseum.org.uk/**
Royal Naval Museum	**www.flagship.org.uk/**
Science Museum	**www.nmsi.ac.uk/**
Sherlock Holmes Museum	**www.sherlock-holmes.co.uk/**
Sikh Museum	**www.sikhmuseum.org/**
Smithsonian Institution	**www.si.edu/**
The Tech Museum of Innovation	**www.thetech.org/**
Victoria and Albert Museum	**www.nal.vam.ac.uk/**

Universities

There is no shortage of colleges and universities across the world at which you can further your studies. These are just some from Australia, New Zealand, UK and the US.

Aberdeen University (UK)	www.abdn.ac.uk/
Aberystwyth University (UK)	www.aber.ac.uk/
Aston University (UK)	www.aston.ac.uk/
Australian National University (AU)	www.anu.edu.au/
Bath University (UK)	www.bath.ac.uk/
Bible College of Victoria (AU)	www.bcv.aus.net/
Birmingham University (UK)	www.birmingham.ac.uk/
Bradford University (UK)	www.bradford.ac.uk/
Bristol University (UK)	www.bris.ac.uk/
Brunel University (UK)	www.brunel.ac.uk/
California State University (US)	www.csuchico.edu/
Canberra Institute of Technology (AU)	www.cit.act.edu.au/
Cardiff University (UK)	www.cf.ac.uk/
Central Institute of Technology (NZ)	www.cit.ac.nz/
Central Queensland University (AU)	www.cqu.edu.au/
Christchurch Polytechnic (NZ)	www.chchp.ac.nz/
City University of New York (US)	www.cuny.edu/
Colorado State University (US)	www.colostate.edu/

Dundee University (UK)	www.dundee.ac.uk/
Durham University (UK)	www.durham.ac.uk/
Essex University (UK)	www.sx.ac.uk/
Exeter University (UK)	www.exeter.ac.uk/
Florida State University (US)	www.fsu.edu/
Glasgow University (UK)	www.gla.ac.uk/
Global Virtual University (NZ)	www.gvu.ac.nz/
Guildhall London (UK)	www.lgu.ac.uk/
Harvard University (US)	www.harvard.edu/
Hull University (UK)	www.hull.ac.uk/
Imperial College (UK)	www.ic.ac.uk/
Indiana University (US)	www.indiana.edu/
International Pacific College (AU)	www.ipca.edu.au/
International Pacific College (NZ)	www.ipc.ac.nz/
James Cook University of North Queensland (AU)	www.jcu.edu.au/
Kansas University (US)	www.ukans.edu/
Keele University (UK)	www.keele.ac.uk/
Leeds University (UK)	www.leeds.ac.uk/
Lincoln University (NZ)	www.lincoln.ac.nz/
Liverpool University (UK)	www.liv.ac.uk/
London Business School (UK)	www.lbs.ac.uk/
London School of Economics (UK)	www.lse.ac.uk/
London University (UK)	www.lon.ac.uk/
Manchester University (UK)	www.man.ac.uk/

Massachusetts Institute of   **www.mit.edu/**
Technology (US)

New York University (US)   **www.nyu.edu/**
Newcastle University (UK)   **www.ncl.ac.uk/**
North Adelaide School of Art (AU) **www.artelaide.com.au/nasa/**
Nottingham University (UK)   **www.nott.ac.uk/**
Open Learning Australia (AU)   **www.ola.edu.au/**
Open University (UK)   **www.open.ac.uk/**
Oxford University (UK)   **www.ox.ac.uk/**
Princeton University (US)   **www.princeton.edu/**
Queens (UK)   **www.qub.ac.uk/**

Queensland University of Technology (AU)	www.qut.edu.au/
Reading University (UK)	www.reading.ac.uk/
Royal Melbourne Institute of Technology (AU)	www.rmit.edu.au/
Sheffield University (UK)	www.shef.ac.uk/
Southampton University (UK)	www.soton.ac.uk/
St Andrews University (UK)	www.st-and.ac.uk/
Stanford University (US)	www.stanford.edu/
Stirling University (UK)	www.stir.ac.uk/
Surrey University (UK)	www.surrey.ac.uk/
Sussex University (UK)	www.sussex.ac.uk/
Swansea University (UK)	www.swan.ac.uk/

| Trinity College (AU) | www.trinity.unimelb.edu.au/ |

UC Berkeley (US)   **www.berkeley.edu/**
UCLA (US)   **www.ucla.edu/**

University of Adelaide (AU)   **www.adelaide.edu.au/**
University of Auckland (NZ)   **www.auckland.ac.nz/**
University of California,   **www.uci.edu/**
Irvine (US)
University of California,   **www.ucr.edu/**
Riverside (US)
University of California,   **www.ucsb.edu/**
Santa Barbara (US)
University of Cambridge (UK)   **www.cam.ac.uk/**

University of Canterbury (NZ)	www.canterbury.ac.nz/
University of Chicago (US)	www.uchicago.edu/
University of Edinburgh (UK)	www.ed.ac.uk/
University of Melbourne (AU)	www.unimelb.edu.au/
University of New England (AU)	www.une.edu.au/
University of New South Wales (AU)	www.unsw.edu.au/
University of Newcastle (AU)	www.newcastle.edu.au/
University of Queensland (AU)	www.uq.edu.au/
University of South Australia (AU)	www.unisa.edu.au/
University of Southern Queensland (AU)	www.usq.edu.au/

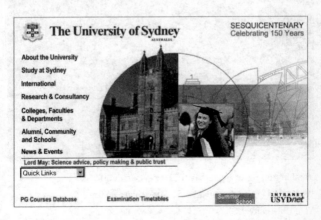

University of Sydney (AU)   www.usyd.edu.au/

University of Tasmania (AU)	**info.utas.edu.au/**
University of Washington (US)	**www.washington.edu/**
University of Western Australia (AU)	**www.uwa.edu.au/**
University Of Western Sydney (AU)	**www.uws.edu.au/**
Victoria University of Technology (AU)	**www.vu.edu.au/**
Victoria University of Wellington (NZ)	**www.vuw.ac.nz/**
Warwick University (UK)	**www.warwick.ac.uk/**

Washington State University (US)	**www.wsu.edu/**
Wellington Polytechnic (NZ)	**www.wnp.ac.nz/**
Yale University (US)	**www.yale.edu/**
York University (UK)	**www.york.ac.uk/**

Entertainment

Apart from the Internet being entertaining, it can also provide you with help when seeking entertainment.

Booking

Online booking is so easy, it's difficult to understand why people do it any other way.

Buzznet	www.buzznet.com/
Dinenet Menus Online	www.menusonline.com/
E! Online	www.eonline.com/
Electric Minds	www.minds.com/
Entertainment Drive	www.edrive.com/
Epicurious	www.epicurious.com/
Pathfinder	www.pathfinder.com/
Rocktropolis	www.rocktropolis.com/
Salon	www.salonmagazine.com/
The Old Farmer's Almanac	www.almanac.com/
The Onion	www.theonion.com/
Zoloft	www.spectacle.com/

Cinema

I'd never been a great cinema goer, until using the Internet to find out what's on, where it's on and what the films are about. You can also book tickets over the Internet on some of these sites.

A Hot Ticket	www.lastminute.com/lmn/
ABC Cinemas	www.abccinemas.co.uk/
Apollo Cinemas	www.apollocinemas.co.uk/
BBC Online – Asian Films	www.bbc.co.uk/networkasia/film/index.shtml
Bollymania	www.dharms.ndirect.co.uk/
Bollywood Central	www.tcreng.com/bollywood/
Bollywood Movie Database	www.wupper.de/sites/unnet/
British Film Institute	www.bfi.org.uk/
British Films Catalogue	www.britfilms.com/
Cinema Theatre Association	www.cinema-theatre.org.uk/
Cyber Bollywood	www.cyberbollywood.com/
Film and Cinema in London	www.thisislondon.co.uk/html/hottx/film/top_direct.html
Film Finder	www.yell.co.uk/yell/ff/
Film Unlimited Preview	www.filmunlimited.co.uk/
Filmweek	film.reviews.co.uk/
Freepages – Cinema Guide	cinema.scoot.co.uk/
ICU Cinema	www.su.ic.ac.uk/clubsocs/scab/cinema/
Internet Movie Database	uk.imdb.com/

List of U.K. Cinemas	www.aber.ac.uk/~jwp/cinemas/
London International Film School	www.lifs.org.uk/
New York – Quad Cinema	www.quadcinema.com/
Picture House Cinemas	www.picturehouse-cinemas.co.uk/
Scoot – Cinema Guide	cinema.scoot.co.uk/
Showcase Cinemas	www.showcasecinemas.co.uk/
UCI Cinemas	www.uci-cinemas.co.uk
Virgin Net – Cinema Listings	www.virgin.com/net/

Warner Village	www.warnervillage.co.uk/

DVD/Video

Home video is gradually being taken over by DVD which provides a far superior picture and makes it easier to locate a part of the film you want to see. It is also far more durable than video tape.

Black Star Videos   www.blackstar.co.uk/video/
Blockbuster Video   www.blockbuster.co.uk/

British Video Association   www.bva.org.uk/
Choices Direct   www.choicesdirect.co.uk/
Choices Video   www.choicesvideo.co.uk/
Code Free DVD   www.codefreedvd.com/
DVD Empire   www.dvdempire.com/
DVD World   www.dvdworld.co.uk/
DVDnet   www.dvdnet.co.uk/

Jungle.com	www.jungle.com/
Moving Music	www.movingmusic.co.uk/
MTV UK & Ireland	www.mtv.co.uk/
Music Zone	www.musiczone.co.uk/
MVC	www.mvc.co.uk/
Record-X	www.record-x.co.uk/
The Zone	www.thezone.co.uk/
Tower Records	www.towerrecords.co.uk/
Video Shop	www.videoshop.co.uk/
VideoParadise	www.videoparadise.com/
VideoZone	www.videozone.co.uk/

Radio Stations

Video, so the song says, killed the radio star. Not according to these sites.

Amber Radio	www.amber.radio.co.uk/
BBC Radio	www.bbc.co.uk/radio/
BBC Radio 1	www.bbc.co.uk/radio1/
BBC Radio 2	www.bbc.co.uk/radio2/
BBC Radio 3	www.bbc.co.uk/radio3/
BBC Radio 4	www.bbc.co.uk/radio4/
BBC Radio 5 Live	www.bbc.co.uk/radio5live/
Capital FM	www.capitalfm.com/
Capital Gold	www.capitalgold.co.uk/
Classic FM	www.classicfm.com/

Galaxy FM	www.galaxyfm.co.uk/
Jazz FM – 92.2 FM	www.jazzfm.com/
M & B Radio	www.mb-radio.co.uk/
Mobile Radio	www.mobile-radio.co.uk/
RTE Radio One	www.rte.ie/
Virgin Net Radio	www.virgin.net/radio
Virgin Radio	www.virginradio.co.uk/
XFM	xfm.co.uk/

Theatre

There's nothing quite like the theatre, and the Internet can help you find a play or a show and some sites will even allow you to book online.

Aloud.com	www.aloud.com/
Battered Suitcase Theatre Company	www.batteredsuitcase.mcmail .com/
Bloomsbury Theatre	www.ucl.ac.uk/ bloomsburytheatre/
Bristol Old Vic Theatre School	oldvic.drama.ac.uk/
British Theatre	britishtheatre.miningco.com/
Children's Theatre Pages	members.aol.com/theatreuk/
Dress Circle (Musical Theatre)	www.dresscircle.co.uk/
Edinburgh Festival Theatre	www.eft.co.uk/
English Theatre Company	www.lissma.se/etc.html
Highlights in Theatreland	www.msn.co.uk/page/8-59.asp

Hot Tickets (Theatre)

**www.thisislondon.co.uk/html/
hottx/theatre/top_direct.html**

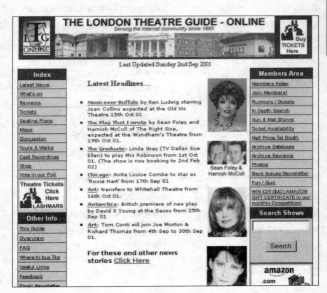

London Theatre Guide   **www.londontheatre.co.uk/**

London Theatre Ticket Sales   **home.clara.net/rap/half/**

London's West End Theatre
Guide   **www.demon.co.uk/
albemarlelondon2/**

National Theatre   **www.nt-online.org/**

New Theatre Publications	www.new-playwrights.demon.co.uk/
Official London Theatre Guide	www.officiallondontheatre.co.uk/
Queen's Film Theatre, Belfast	www.qub.ac.uk/qft/
Royal Lyceum Theatre Company	www.infoser.com/infotheatre/lyceum/
Royal Shakespeare Company	www.rsc.org.uk/
Scene One	www.sceneone.co.uk/s1/theatre
The Globe	www.rdg.ac.uk/acadepts/ln/globe/globe.html
The Stage	www.thestage.co.uk/
Theatre Historical Society of America	www2.hawaii.edu/~angell/thsa/
Theatre Web	www.uktw.co.uk/offers.html
UK Theatre Web	www.uktw.co.uk/
What's On Stage	www.whatsonstage.com/
Workshop Theatre	www.leeds.ac.uk/theatre/foyer.htm

TV

Use these sites to find out what's on and what will be on, and also what was on.

ABC-TV	www.abc-tv.net/
Anglia Television	www.anglia.tv.co.uk/
Anglia Television Online	www.angliatv.co.uk/
BBC Online – Schedules	www.bbc.co.uk/television/

Cable Guide	www.cableguide.co.uk/bread
Challenge TV	www.challengetv.co.uk/
Channel 5 Television	www.channel5.co.uk/
Channel Four	www.channel4.com/
Classic Kids TV	www.geocities.com/ TelevisionCity/1011/
Cult TV	www.metronet.co.uk/cultv/
Cult TV Memorabilia	www.tv-memorabilia.demon .co.uk/links.htm
Discovery Channel Online	www.discovery.com/
EuroTV	www.eurotv.com/
Film 4	www.filmfour.com/
Film and TV Craft and Technology	www.fatcat.co.uk/
Guardian Unlimited – TV Listings	www.guardianunlimited.co.uk/TV/
Independent Television Commission	www.itc.org.uk/
ITV	www.itv.co.uk/
Kaysnet	www.kaysnet.com/
Meridian Broadcasting	www.meridian.tv.co.uk/
Radio Times Guide	www.radiotimes.beeb.com/
Rapture TV	www.rapture.co.uk/
Satellite TV Europe	www.satellite-tv.co.uk/
Sky	www.skynow.co.uk/
Sky Digital	www.sky.com/
Techno TV Systems	www.techno.cpd.co.uk/
Teletext TV Plus	www1.teletext.co.uk/tvplus/

Television Ark	**www.tv-ark.co.uk/**
Thames TV	**www.geocities.com/Hollywood/ 5144/**
Time TV	**www.timetv.co.uk/**

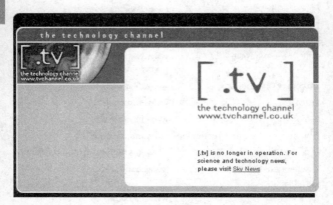

TV	**www.tvchannel.co.uk/**
TV Zone	**www.visimag.com/tvzone/**
UK Terrestrial Cult TV	**members.tripod.com/~ukculttv/**
What's On?	**msn.co.uk/page/8-60.asp**

Web-Radio

You don't need a radio to receive radio. You can get a huge range of radio broadcasts via the Internet.

| 100 Years of Radio Web | **www.alpcom.it/hamradio** |

A Net Station	**www.advice-net.com/**
Boom Booom Net Radio	**www.bmbient.demon.co.uk/ blazznet/**
Broadcast.com	**www.broadcast.com/**
BRS Web Radio	**www.web-radio.com**
First Music	**www.firstmusic.com/radio/**
Galaxy FM	**www.galaxyfm.co.uk/**
Internet Top 40 Countdown	**www.top40countdown.com/**
Live Online	**www.live-online.com/**
Live Radio on the Internet	**www.frodo.u-net.com/radio.htm**
MIT List of Radio Stations	**wmbr.mit.edu/stations/list.html**
Net Radio Links	**www.bodo.com/radio.htm**
NetRadio ISDN Zone	**www.netradio.net/isdn**
NetRadio.com	**www.netradio.net/**
Radio Free Underground	**www.stitch.com/studio/**
Radio Online	**www.radio-online.com/**
Radio Tower	**www.radiotower.com**
Rode Boef Real Web Radio	**www.gironet.nl/home/rodeboef/**
The Wizard Free	**www.imagescape.com/wzrd**

Virgin Net Radio	**www.virgin.com/net/**
WFMU Radio 91.1 FM	**www.wfmu.org**

| Whatsnew.com | www.whatsnew.com/ |
| Zero9 – Radio | www.bionicsite.com/zero9/ |

Web-TV

You can also receive TV programmes via the Internet.

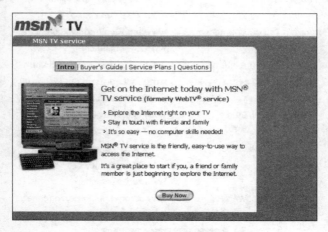

MSN TV	www.msntv.com/
Philips Magnavox Internet TV	www.philipstraining.com/webtv/intv62.html
WebTV FAQ	www.owenmeany.com/faq.html

Finance

Whatever aspect of financial dealings you need to find out about, you'll find it here.

Information

Most financial dealings, including banking, are a complete mystery to most of us. But the Internet can provide advice on virtually every aspect of finance including share dealing and investment.

Bank Rate Monitor	www.bankrate.com/
Credit Report	www.consumerinfo.com/
Day Trader News	www.daytradernews.net/
FinAid	www.finaid.org/
Financial Times	www.ft.com/
FT Your Money	www.ftyourmoney.com/
Infopages	www.infopages.net/
InvestorGuide	www.investorguide.com/
Marketguide	www.marketguide.com/
SmartMoney	www.smartmoney.com/
The Economist	www.economist.com/

The Street.com	**www.thestreet.com/**
Wall Street Journal	**www.wsj.com/**
Yahoo Finance	**biz.yahoo.com/**

Banking

Money makes the world go around, says the song. The trouble with conventional banking is that you can only make the world revolve at certain times. More and more banks are offering 24–hour online banking giving you the opportunity to make transactions and view your account at any time. The only thing you have to visit the bank for is to withdraw hard cash.

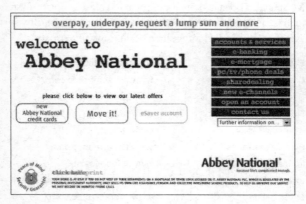

| Abbey National Group | **www.abbeynational.co.uk/** |
| American Express | **www.americanexpress.com/** |

American Savings Bank	www.asbhawaii.com/
Banco Central Do Brasil	www.bcb.gov.br/
Bank of America	www.bankofamerica.com/
Bank of Cleveland	www.bankofcleveland.com/
Bank of Estonia	www.ee/epbe/en/
Bank of Finland	www.bof.fi/
Bank of Ireland	www.bank-of-ireland.co.uk/
Bank of Israel	www.bankisrael.gov.il/
Bank of Japan	www.boj.or.jp/
Bank of Latvia	www.bank.lv/
Bank of Lebanon	www.bdl.gov.lb/
Bank of Lithuania	www.lbank.lt/
Bank of Mexico	www.banxico.org.mx/
Bank of Montreal	www.bmo.com/
Bank of Mozambique	www.bancomoc.mz/
Bank of New York	www.bankofny.com/
Bank of Newport	www.bankofnewport.com/
Bank of Papa New Guinea	www.datec.com.pg/
Bank of Portugal	www.bportugal.pt/
Bank of Scotland	www.bankofscotland.co.uk/
Bank of Slovenia	www.bsi.si/
Bank of Thailand	www.bot.or.th/
Bank of Wales	www.bankofwales.co.uk/
Bank of Zambia	www.boz.zm/
Bank One	www.bankone.com

Banque de France	www.banque-france.fr/
Barclays Bank	www.barclays.co.uk/
Bermuda Monetary Authority	www.bma.bm/
Bulgarian National Bank	www.bnb.bg/
Capital Bank	www.capitalbank.co.uk/
Central Bank of Armenia	www.cba.am/
Central Bank of Barbados	www.centralbank.org.bb/
Central Bank of Bosnia	www.cbbh.gov.ba/
Central Bank of Chile	www.bcentral.cl/
Central Bank of China	www.cbc.gov.tw/
Central Bank of Cyprus	www.centralbank.gov.cy/
Central Bank of Iceland	www.sedlabanki.is/
Central Bank of Jordan	www.cbj.gov.jo/
Central Bank of Malta	www.centralbankmalta.com/
Central Bank of Swaziland	www.centralbank.sz/
Central Bank of the Netherlands Antilles	centralbank.an/
Central Bank of the Republic of Turkey	www.tcmb.gov.tr/
Central Bank of Trinidad and Tobago	www.central-bank.org.tt/
Central Bank of Uruguay	www.bcu.gub.uy/
Chase Manhattan Bank	www.chase.com/
Citibank (UK)	www.citibank.com/uk/
Citibank (US)	www.citibank.com/
Columbia Bank	www.columbiabank.com/

Co-operative Bank, The	**www.co-operativebank.co.uk/**
Croatian National Bank	**www.hnb.hr/sadr.htm**
Czech National Bank	**www.cnb.cz/en/**
De Nederlandsche Bank	**www.dnb.nl/**
Deutsche Genossenschaftsbank	**www.dgbank.de/**
Eastern Caribbean Central Bank	**www.eccb-centralbank.org/**
Egg	**www.egg.com/**
Federal Reserve Bank	**www.kc.frb.org/**
First American Bank	**www.firstambank.com/**

firstdirect.com

Log on...

first direct

▶ about us
▶ bank
  ▶ banking
  ▶ insurance
  ▶ travel

▶ click here to join

First Direct	www.firstdirect.com/
First Republic Bank	www.firstrepublic.com/
First Union	www.firstunion.com/
Halifax Bank	www.halifax.co.uk/
Houston Savings Bank	www.houstonsavings.com/
HSBC	www.banking.hsbc.co.uk/
JP Morgan & Co. Incorporated	www.jpmorgan.com/
Legal & General	www.landg.com/
Lloyds TSB	www.lloydstsb.co.uk/
Monetary and Foreign Exchange Authority of Macau	amcm.macau.gov.mo/
Monetary Authority of Singapore	www.mas.gov.sg/
National Australia Bank	www.national.com.au/
National Bank of Moldova	www.bnm.org/
National Bank of the Republic of Macedonia	www.nbrm.gov.mk/
National Savings	www.nationalsavings.co.uk/
National Westminster Bank	www.natwest.co.uk/
NationsBank	www.nationsbank.com/
Nationwide	www.nationwide.co.uk/

North Korean Financial Institutions	www.kimsoft.com/korea/
Northern Rock	www.northernrock.co.uk/
Oesterreichische Nationalbank	www.oenb.co.at/
Reserve Bank of Australia	www.rba.gov.au/
Reserve Bank of NZ	www.rbnz.govt.nz/
Royal Bank of Scotland	www.rbs.co.uk/
Smile	www.smile.co.uk/
Standard Bank	www.sboff.com/
Swiss National Bank	www.snb.ch/
UniCredito Italiano	www.credit.it/
US Trust Boston	www.ustrustboston.com/
Virgin Direct	www.virgin-direct.co.uk/
Washington Mutual	www.washingtonmutual.com/
Woolwich	www.woolwich.co.uk/

Investments

Making your money work for you seems to be more important than ever to ensure a reasonable degree of comfort in later years. But beware – prices can fall as well as rise.

Aberdeen Technology	www.aberdeen-asset.com/
Bloomberg Markets	www.bloomberg.com/uk/markets/
Check Free Investment Services	www.secapl.com/
CNBC	www.cnbc.com/

CNN Financial Network	www.cnnfn.com/
Cyber Cash	www.cybercash.com/
Datek	www.datek.com/
Dow Jones	www.dowjones.com/
Fidelity	www.fidelity.co.uk/
Fidelity Investments	www.fidelity.com/
Ft.com	www.ft.com/
FTSE International	www.ftse.com/
Individual Investor	www.individualinvestor.com/
IMoney Manager	www.moneymanager.com.au/
Investco GT	www.tel.hr/investco/
Jupiter Income Trust	www.jupiteronline.co.uk/
London Stock Exchange	www.londonstockex.co.uk/
Money Online	www.money.com/
Money Scope	abcnews.go.com/sections/business/
MSN Money	money.msn.co.uk/
Nasdaq	www.nasdaq.com/
Personal Wealth	www.personalwealth.com/
Prudential	www.prudential.com/
Quicken.com	www.quicken.com/
Quote.com	www.quote.com/
Save & Prosper	www.prosper.co.uk/
Stockmarket	www.moneyworld.co.uk/stocks/

TELE
SH▯RE
ONLINE

FOR ALL THE LATEST NEWS AND REAL-TIME SHARE
PRICES BY TELEPHONE CALL TELESHARE
CLICK HERE OR CALL 08705 212223 FOR A FREE USER GUIDE

Frankfurt (DAX) 5361.6 (+49.5) London (FTSE-100) 1609.70 (+15.80) NASDAQ (Nasdaq-100) 6605.20 (+35.40)

Teleshare	www.teleshare.co.uk/
The Motley Fool	www.fool.com/
Threadneedle	www.threadneedle.co.uk/
UK-iNvest	www.uk-invest.com/
UK Share Net	www.uksharenet.com/
Waterhouse Securities Inc.	www.waterhouse.com/

Loans

There never seems to be any shortage of people who are prepared
to offer to lend you money. If you do need to borrow, it makes
sense to shop around for the best deal.

AccuBanc Mortgage Corporation	www.accubanc.com/
Anchor Mortgage	www.anchormortgage.com/
APT Funding	www.aptfunding.com/
Besthomeloan.com	www.besthomeloan.com/
Capstead Mortgage Corporation	www.capstead.com/
Carloan.com	www.carloan.com/
Century Oak	www.centuryoak.com/
CMI Mortgage info	www.cmi-mortgageinfo.com/
Dominion Corporation	www.dominfin.com/
E-Loan	www.eloan.com/
E-Mortage1	www.e-mortgage1.com/

EMFinance	**www.emfinance.com**/
GetSmart	**www.getsmart.com**/
GSF mortgage	**www.gsf-mortgage.com**/

HFC	**www.hfc.com**/
Home Owners.com	**www.homeowners.com**/
I Promise	**www.ipromise.co.uk**/
Insignia Financial Group	**www.insigniafinancial.com**/
Loan Web	**www.loanweb.com**/
Loanapp.com	**www.loanapp.com**/
Microsurf Internet Services	**www.microsurf.com**/
Mid-Atlantic Financial Group	**www.ihomeloans.com**/
Money Hunter	**www.moneyhunter.com**/
Mortgage Direct	**www.mortgagedirect.com**/

Mortgage Edge	www.mortgageedge.com/
Mortgage Market Information Services	www.interest.com/
Mortgage Resource	www.mortgage-resource.com/
Mortgage Select	www.mortgageselect.com/
Mortgage101.com	www.mortgage101.com/
Mortgage-Net	www.mortgage-net.com/

Nationwide	www.nationwide.co.uk/
Northern Rock	www.northernrock.co.uk/
Norwest Corporation Personal Loans	www.ntrs.com/is/
Norwest Online	www.norwest.com/
RMCVanguard	www.rmcv.com/
Standard Life	www.standardlifebank.com/

The Mortgage Network	www.themortgagenetwork.com/
The Mortgage Outlet	www.themortgageoutlet.com/
Worldloan.com	www.worldloan.com/

Share Trading

Some people make their living buying and selling shares. The Internet has made the task considerably easier by providing up-to-the minute prices.

| American Stock Exchange | www.amex.com/ |

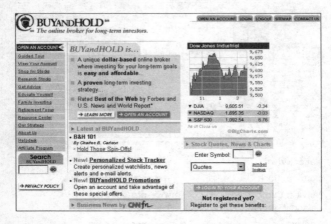

| Buy and Hold | www.buyandhold.com/ |
| Charting UK Shares | www.metronet.co.uk/bigwood/shares/ |

Check Your Shares	www.msn.co.uk/page/12-88.asp
Citywire	www.citywire.co.uk/
CMC Group	www.forex-cmc.co.uk/
CMC Group	www.cmcplc.com/
Copenhagen Stock Exchange	www.xcse.dk/uk/
E*Trade	www.etrade.com/
E*Trade (UK)	www.etrade.co.uk/

Ellis & Partners Ltd	www.ellisandpartners.co.uk/
Interactive Investor International	www.iii.co.uk/
Internet Stock Report	www.internetnews.com/stocks/
London Stock Exchange	www.londonstockex.co.uk/
Malcolm Hills	www.powerup.com.au/~mhills/mal1.htm
Motley Fool UK	www.fool.co.uk/
Nasdaq UK	www.nasdaq-uk.com/
New York Stock Exchange	www.nyse.com/
NO Global Markets	www.ino.com/
Stockmarket	www.moneyworld.co.uk/stocks/

StockMaster   www.stockmaster.com/

StockSelector.com   www.stockselector.com/

Stocktrade   www.stocktrade.co.uk/

Teleshare   www.teleshare.co.uk/

The Share Centre   www.share.co.uk/

The Share Centre   www.share.com/

UK-iNvest.com   www.uk-invest.com/

Virtual Stock Exchange   www.virtualstockexchange.com/

Wall Street City   www.wallstreetcity.com/

Xest   www.xest.com/

Food & Drink

I'm always amazed that people want to make such a meal out of having a meal. Even to the extent of spending half a day preparing it and then inviting friends around in the evening to consume it. Food is simply fuel for our bodies. It's a good thing that we don't hold a party every time the car needs petrol.

Drinks

These sites all have one thing in common: sampling their contents can leave you in no fit state to operate a computer.

About Scotch Whisky	www.scotchwhisky.com/
Absolut Vodka	www.absolutvodka.com/
ACATS Internet Bar Pages	www.epact.se/acats/
Alcohol	www.mindbodysoul.gov.uk/ alcohol/alcmenu.htm
Allied Domecq	www.allieddomecqplc.com/
Bacardi	www.bacardi.com/
Baileys PleasureDome	www.baileys.com/
Beer & Pubs UK	www.blra.co.uk/

Beerstalker	www.beerstalker.co.uk/
Breweriana – Pub paraphernalia	www.eagle.co.uk/breweriana
BreWorld	www.breworld.com/
Bulmers	www.bulmer.com/
Canadian Mist	www.canadianmist.com/
Captain Morgan Rum	www.rum.com/
Chivas Regal	www.chivas.com/
Cider and Perry Recipes	web.bham.ac.uk/GraftonG/cider/recipes.htm

Cider Surfers Arms	www.cidersurfersarms.com/
Courvoisier	www.courvoisier.com/
Diageo	www.diageo.co.uk/
Drink Store	www.drinkstore.com
DrinkBoy	www.drinkboy.com/

Dunkertons Cider Company	www.kc3ltd.co.uk/business/dunker.html
Edinburgh Malt Whisky Tour	www.dcs.ed.ac.uk/home/jhb/whisky/hitrail.html
Epicurious Drinking	food.epicurious.com/d_drinking/d00_home/drinking.html
Food and Drink – Wine Course	www.bbc.co.uk/foodanddrink/
Grand Marnier	www.grand-marnier.com/
Hop Back Brewery	www.hopback.co.uk/
Jack Daniels	www.jackdaniels.com/
Jamaica Standard Products	www.caribplace.com/foods/jspcl.htm
Last Call	www.lstcall.com
Mad About Wine	www1.madaboutwine.com/
Millennium – Drinking Game	www.ecis.com/~weasel/millennium.txt
Now 365	www.now365.com/
Pub World	www.pubworld.co.uk/
Red Dwarf – Drinking Game	www2.hunterlink.net.au/~dejmb/rd_drink.htm
Scotch Doc	www.scotchdoc.com/
Simply Food – Wine	www.simplyfood.co.uk/glug/
Stoli Central	www.stoli.com/
Tetley's Bitter	www.smoothlydoesit.co.uk/
Think About Drink	www.wrecked.co.uk/
Victoria Wine	www.victoriawine.co.uk/

Mixing Drinks

Should it be shaken or stirred? Mixing cocktails is quite an art, I understand. Apparently not the actual pouring of assortments of brightly coloured liquids into a pot, it's the bottle juggling that really makes a good cocktail waiter.

Bar Drinks	www.bardrinks.com/
Cecilia's Book of Martinis	www.brecknet.com/cecilias/martini.html
Cocktail	www.hotwired.com/cocktail
Cocktail Culture	www.geocities.com/Paris/5289/cocktail.html
Cocktail.com	www.cocktail.com/ski/
Cocktails	cocktails.miningco.com/
Cocktails Central	www.smworld.co.uk/cocktails/
Homemade Drink Recipes	www.inforamp.net/~mcdermot/drinks.html
Making Liqueurs and Cordials at Home	www.lusionspub.com/
Perfect Martini	www.reville.com/martini.html
Swank-O-Rama: Cocktail Revolution	www.cyborganic.com/People/jpmckay
The Ultimate Bar Guide	home.earthlink.net/~schimster/
Traditional Cocktail Recipes	www.laboheme.cz/cocktails.htm
Webtender	www.webtender.com/specials/xmas

Soft Drinks

It's best to keep off the hard stuff – it's not good for you. It's much better to stick to drinks which are packed out with sugar and ingredients that are identified with an 'e' number.

The Beverage Network	www.thebevnet.com/
Coca-Cola	www.cocacola.com/
Dr Pepper	www.drpepper.com/
Mello Yello	www.melloyello.com
Mr Pibb!	bluWeb.com/us/chouser/info/pibb/
National Soft Drink Association	www.nsda.org/
OK Soda	spleen.mit.edu/ok.html
Tizer	www.tizer.co.uk/
Wet Planet Beverages	www.joltcola.com/

Fast Food

Sometimes it's preferable not to have to do the washing up. Many of these popular eating houses have a similar philosophy.

A&W Rootbeer	www.a-wrootbeer.com/
Arby's	www.arbysrestaurants.com/
Back Yard Burgers	www.backyardburgers.com/
Baker's Drive Thru	www.bakersdrivethru.com/
Blimpie	www.blimpie.com/
Burger King	www.burgerking.com/

Chick-Fil-A	www.chickfila.com/
Churchs Chicken	www.churchs.com/
Dairy Queen	www.dairyqueen.com/
Fast Food Facts	www.olen.com/food/book.html
Interactive Food Finder	www.olen.com/food/

KFC	www.kfc.com/
Koo Koo Roo	www.kookooroo.com/
Long John Silver's	www.ljsilvers.com/
McDonald's	www.mcdonalds.com/
Panda Express	www.pandaexpress.com/
Pizza Hut	www.pizzahut.com/
Popeye's Chicken	www.popeyes.com/
Poquito Mas	www.poquitomas.com/
Quizno's	www.quiznos.com/
Sonic	www.sonicdrivein.com/
Taco Time	www.tacotime.com/
Tubby's Grilled Submarines	www.tubby.com/
Wendy's International	www.wendys.com/
White Castle	www.whitecastle.com/
World Wrapps	www.worldwrapps.com/

Home Cooking

I specialise in things that come out of tins. If you want to develop beyond that stage, visit some of these sites which offer lots of help for the beginner or the expert and some excellent recipes.

A la Carte TV	www.alacartetv.com/
Albertsons	www.albertsons.com/
AllRecipes.com	www.allrecipes.com/
American Foods	www.americanfoods.com/
Better Baking	www.betterbaking.com/
Betty Crocker	www.bettycrocker.com/
CD Kitchen	www.cdkitchen.com/
Chefs Catalog	www.chefscatalog.com/
Chefs-store	www.chefs-store.com/
Cheftalk	www.cheftalk.com/
Chetday	www.chetday.com/
Chicken Recipe	www.chickenrecipe.com/
Cookbooks	www.cookbooks.com/
Cookie Recipe	www.cookierecipe.com/
Cooking Compass	www.cookingcompass.com/
Cooking Light	www.cookinglight.com/
Cooking With Kids	www.cookingwithkids.com/
Cooking.com	www.cooking.com/
Cooks Illustrated	www.cooksillustrated.com/
Cuisinenet	www.cuisinenet.com/
Culinary Café	www.culinarycafe.com/

Culinary Pleasures	www.culinarypleasures.com/
Culinary.com	www.culinary.com/
Culinary.net	www.culinary.net/
CulinaryChef.Com	www.culinarychef.com/
Cutlery	www.cutlery.com/
Cyberdiet	www.cyberdiet.com/
Dean de Luca	www.deandeluca.com/
Delicious India	www.deliciousindia.com/
Diabetic Gourmet	www.diabeticgourmet.com/
Eat.com	www.eat.com/
eHow.com	www.ehow.com/
Epicurean	www.epicurean.com/
Epicurious	www.epicurious.com/
Epicurus.com	www.epicurus.com/
Fatfree.com	www.fatfree.com/
Food	www.food.com/
Food Consultants	www.foodconsultants.com/
Food Institute.com	www.foodinstitute.com/
Food Safety	www.foodsafety.gov/
Food TV	www.foodtv.com/
Foodvision	www.foodvision.com/
French Culinary	www.frenchculinary.com/
Gist	www.gist.com/
Global Gourmet	www.globalgourmet.com/
Good Cooking	www.goodcooking.com/

Gourmet Connection	www.gourmetconnection.com/
Gourmet Market	www.gourmetmarket.com/
Happy Cookers	www.happycookers.com/
Healthy Eating	www.healthy-eating.com/
HGTV	www.hgtv.com/
Homearts.com	www.homearts.com/
Homechef	www.homechef.com/
iChef.com	www.ichef.com/
India Tastes	www.indiatastes.com/
Kitchen Emporium	www.kitchenemporium.com/
Kitchenlink	www.kitchenlink.com/
Lets eat oc.com	www.letseatoc.com/
Living Foods	www.living-foods.com/
Martha Stewart	www.marthastewart.com/
Merry Christmas.com	merry-christmas.com/recipes.htm
Minute Meals	www.minutemeals.com/
Mollie Katzen	www.molliekatzen.com/
Mosiman Academy	www.mosiman.com/
My Meals	www.my-meals.com/
My-Recipe.com	www.my-recipe.com/
Outlaw Cook	www.outlawcook.com/
Pastrywiz	www.pastrywiz.com/
Peapod.com	www.peapod.com/
Pillsbury	www.pillsbury.com/
Recipe	www.recipe.com/

Recipe a Day	www.recipe-a-day.com/
Recipe World	www.recipe-world.com/
Recipe Xchange	www.recipexchange.com/
Recipes Archive: Preserving	recipes.taronga.com/preserving/
Recipes Today	www.recipestoday.com/
SaladRecipe.com	www.saladrecipe.com/
Simply Food	www.simplyfood.co.uk/
Soup Recipe	www.souprecipe.com/
Star Chefs	www.starchefs.com/
Starbucks	www.starbucks.com/
Tavolo	www.tavolo.com/
Texas Cooking	www.texascooking.com/
The Food Web	www.thefoodweb.com/
Top Secret Recipes	www.topsecretrecipes.com/
Ucook.com	www.ucook.com/
Vegetable Patch, The	www.vegetablepatch.net/
Vegetarian Society	www.vegsoc.org/
Veggies Unite	www.vegweb.com/food/
Vegkitchen.com	www.vegkitchen.com/
Vegweb	www.vegweb.com/
Webvan	www.webvan.com/
Your Kitchen	www.your-kitchen.com/
Yum Yum	www.yumyum.com/

Ingredients

You can't make anything without the ingredients. These sites have lots of them and lots of tips about what to do with them.

Alaska Seafood Marketing Institute	www.alaskaseafood.org/
Crate and Barrel	www.crateandbarrel.com/
Eat Chicken	www.eatchicken.com/
Foodline	www.foodline.com/
Home Grocer	www.homegrocer.com/
I love pasta	www.ilovepasta.org/
Net Grocer	www.netgrocer.com/

Our Daily Bread - Eat Healthy - Eat Vegan

Food & Fun PastryWiz — Chocolate — Click for Cake

Browse by Category or Ingredient

Our Daily Bread	www.our-daily-bread.com/
Schwans	www.schwans.com/
Send.com	www.send.com/
Shoprite	www.shoprite.com/
Sweet Lobster	www.sweetlobster.com/
Tuna	www.tunaking.com/
Why Milk?	www.whymilk.com/
Zagats.com	www.zagats.com/

Supermarkets

More and more supermarkets are offering online ordering for the weekly groceries. You have to plan in advance to ensure there is a 'delivery slot' at a time when someone can be at home to receive them.

ABCO Foods	www.abcofoods.com/
Acme Markets	www.acmemarkets.com/
Asda	www.asda.co.uk/
Food City	www.foodcity.com/
Food Ferry	www.foodferry.co.uk/
FoodFare	www.foodfare.com/
Harrods Online	www.harrods.com/
Online British Foodstore	www.3ex.com/
Pathmark Stores	www.pathmark.com/
Pavilions	www.pavilions.com/
PC Foods	www.pcfoods.com/
Price Chopper Supermarkets	www.pricechopper.com/
Safeway	www.safeway.com/
Sainsbury's	www.sainsburystoyou.co.uk/
Shaw's Supermarkets	www.shaws.com/
Somerfield	www.somerfield.co.uk/
Tesco	www.tesco.co.uk/software/
ValuPage	www.supermarkets.com/
Waitrose Supermarkets	www.waitrose.co.uk/
Woolworths	www.woolworths.co.uk/

Government & Politics

There are lots of sites relating to the powers that be from all countries. Many of these sites have links to other sites within the same government-run organisation.

Government

It's comforting to know that the people charged with making decisions about our lives are so accessible.

Australian Commonwealth Government	**www.fed.gov.au/**
British Governments & Elections	**www.psr.keele.ac.uk/area/uk/ uktable.htm**
Cabinet Office	**www.cabinet-office.gov.uk/**
Canadian Government	**canada.gc.ca/**
CCTA Government Information Service	**www.open.gov.uk/**
Criminal Justice System	**www.criminal-justice-system.gov.uk/**
Falkland Islands Government	**www.falklands.gov.fk/**

GCHQ Government Communications HQ	www.fas.org/irp/world/uk/gchq/
Government Agencies	www.ngfl.gov.uk/ngfl/govern/ gov_agency_list.html
Her Majesty Queen Elizabeth II	canada.gc.ca/howgoc/queen/ quind_e.html
Information from the Irish State	www.irlgov.ie/
Isle of Man Government	www.gov.im/
New Zealand Government	www.govt.nz/
Scottish Local Government Index	www.oultwood.com/localgov/ scotland.htm
The White House	www.whitehouse.gov/
UK Government Communications HQ	www.gchq.gov.uk/
UK Local Government Index	www.oultwood.com/localgov/ england.htm
UK Public Services and Local Government	www.hants.gov.uk/services.html
UK Royal Family	www.royal.gov.uk/
UK Taxation Directory	www.uktax.demon.co.uk/ home.htm
US Government	www.government.com/
US Government and Regulatory Bodies	www.pharmweb.net/pwmirror/ pwk/pharmwebk.html
Welsh Local Government Index	www.oultwood.com/localgov/ wales.htm

Politics

Politicians are a very special breed of people: they all seem to have the ability to answer a question without actually answering it.

All Politics	www.allpolitics.com/
Australian Labour Party	www.alp.org.au/
Australian Parliament	www.aph.gov.au/
Australian Politics	ccadfa.cc.adfa.oz.au/~adm/politics/politics.html
Australian Republican Movement	www.republic.org.au/
British Party Websites	www.psr.keele.ac.uk/area/uk/localweb.htm
British Politics	www.ukpol.co.uk/
British Politics	www.geocities.com/CapitolHill/Lobby/5436/
Christian Democratic Party	www.cda.nl/
Communist Party USA	www.hartford-hwp.com/cp-usa/
Conservative Party (UK)	www.conservative-party.org.uk/
Conservative US Politics	usconservatives.about.com/
Democratic National Committee	www.democrats.org/
Election Results	www.election.demon.co.uk/election.html
ePolitix	www.epolitix.com/
Guardian Unlimited – Politics	politics.guardian.co.uk/
Green Parties Worldwide	www.greens.org/
Houses of Parliament	www.parliament.uk/

Institute of World Politics	www.iwp.edu/
Labour Party (UK)	www.labour.org.uk/
Liberal Democrats Party (UK)	www.libparty.demon.co.uk/
Liberal US Politics	usliberals.about.com/
New Communist Party	www.geocities.com/CapitolHill/2853/
No. 10 Downing Street	www.number-10.gov.uk/
Political Corruption	www.ex.ac.uk/~RDavies/arian/scandals/political.html
Political Parties	www.4politicalparties.com/
Politics.com	www.politics.com/
Probe Ministries	www.probe.org/
Reform Party	www.reformparty.org/
Republican National Committee	www.rnc.org/
Republican Party	www.fiannafail.ie/
Sinn Fein	sinnfein.ie/
The Australian Democrats	www.democrats.org.au/
The Conservative Party	www.conservative-party.org.uk/
UK Economics & Politics	dspace.dial.pipex.com/geoff.riley/
UK Politics Brief	www.ukpoliticsbrief.co.uk/
US Politics	uspolitics.about.com/
Westminster Watch	www.westminsterwatch.co.uk/

Health

Personally, I'm not sure whether it is a good idea to provide medical material to laymen – it could lead to hypochondria. These websites are packed with information about staying healthy and how to heal yourself. It should be stressed that if you are unwell, your GP should be consulted, not your favourite website.

Alternative Medicine

Some people swear by it, others dismiss it as hocus-pocus. Perhaps the safest stance is to place it somewhere between those two extremes. Indeed alternative medicine is frequently referred to as complementary medicine meaning that it can be used alongside, but should not replace, conventional medicine.

Acupuncture.com	www.acupuncture.com/
Acupuncture References	www.americanwholehealth.com/
Acupuntura	www.acupuntura.org/
All Herb	www.allherb.com/
American Apitherapy Society	www.apitherapy.org/
American Back Society	www.americanbacksoc.org/

Aroma Direct	www.aromagift.com/
Bhakti Yoga	www.webcom.com/~ara/
British School of Homoeopathy	www.homoeopathy.co.uk/
Buteyko Asthma Education	www.buteyko-usa.com/
Buteyko Breath Reconditioning Technique	www.wt.com.au/~pkolb/buteyko.htm
Buteyko Health Centre	www.buteyko.com/
Buteyko Institute of Breathing & Health	www.buteyko.com.au/
Buteyko Method	www.buteykovideo.com/
Buteyko Online	www.buteyko.co.nz/
Canadian Chiropractic Association	www.ccachiro.org/
Canadian Neuro-Optic Research Institute	www.cnri.edu/
Causal Kinesiology	www.kineko.com/
Chiropractors' Association of Australia Ltd	www.caa.com.au/
Dan Tao, The Way of Transformation	www.erols.com/dantao/
Foundation for Trad. Chinese Medicine	www.ftcm.freeserve.co.uk/
Guide to Aromatherapy	www.fragrant.demon.co.uk/
Guide to Transcendental Meditation	www.tm.org/
Health Kinesiology UK	www.healthk.co.uk/
Herb and Juice Stop	www.mindspring.com/~morfil/shop.htm

Homeo Doctor	www.tiruchicity.com/homeo
Homeopath	www.homeopath.co.uk/
Homeopathic Drugs	community.net/~neils/faqhom.html

Institute for Classical Homoeopathy	www.classicalhomoeopathy.org/
International Chiropractic Pediatric Assoc.	www.4icpa.org/
International Chiropractors Association	www.chiropractic.org/
International Federation of Aromatherapists	www.ifa.org.au/
International Trepanation Advocacy Group	www.trepan.com/
Introduction to Aromatherapy	www.eclipse.co.uk/iys/
Karma Yoga: Path of Selfless Action	www.talamasca.org/avatar/yoga3.html
Lanes Health	www.laneshealth.com/
Oasis By Design	www.angelfire.com/hi/oasisbydesign/

General Health

All of us should look after our bodies and, with care, they'll last a lifetime. From your head to your toes, and all parts between, there is no shortage of advice on the Internet.

A–Z of Vitamins and Minerals	www.surgerydoor.co.uk/level1/vitamins.shtml
American Heart	www.americanheart.org/
Body, The	www.thebody.com/
BUPA	www.bupa.co.uk/
Department of Health	www.doh.gov.uk/
First Aid	firstaid.ie.eu.org/
Fitness Online	www.fitnessonline.com/
Food Additives	www.faia.org.uk/
Health	www.health.org/
Health Central	www.healthcentral.com/
Health Development Agency	www.hda-online.org.uk/
Health Matters	www.healthmatters.org.uk/
Healthatoz	www.healthatoz.com/
Healthfinder	www.healthfinder.gov/
HealthIndex UK	www.healthindex.co.uk/
Healthshop	www.healthshop.com/
Healthworks	www.healthworks.co.uk/
Intelihealth	www.intelihealth.com/
Managing Stress	www.managingstress.com/
Medicare	www.medicare.gov/

Medscape	www.medscape.com/
Mind, Body & Soul	www.mindbodysoul.gov.uk/
NetDoctor	www.netdoctor.co.uk/
NHS Direct	www.nhsdirect.nhs.uk/
Nutravida	www.nutravida.com/
Self Care	www.selfcare.com/
Surgery Door	www.surgerydoor.co.uk/
UK Health Centre	www.healthcentre.org.uk/
Vegetarian Society	www.vegsoc.org/
Vitamins & Health	www.vitaminsandhealth.co.uk/
Web MD	www.webmd.com/
Wellbeing	www.wellbeing.com/
Your Health	www.yourhealth.com/

Medicine

You can buy your medicines over the Internet as well as get advice on their use.

| Drug Library | www.druglibrary.org/ |
| Drugstore | www.drugstore.com/ |

| Pharmacy2U | www.pharmacy2u.co.uk/ |

Parenting

The problem we found when bringing up children is that seemingly every other parent in the world thinks they are the experts. The way they did it was right for their child and will, therefore, be right for every other child and if you do it a different way, you're wrong. Some websites fall into that category but there are many more which will offer sound unbiased advice based on tried and trusted methods.

AAP	**www.aap.org/**
Baby World	**www.babyworld.co.uk/**
BBC Education – Pregnancy	**www.bbc.co.uk/education/ health/parenting/pregnant.shtml**
Breastfeeding & Childbirth	**www.breastfeeding.co.uk/**
British Pregnancy Advisory Service	**www.bpas.demon.co.uk/**
Childcare Now!	**www.childcare-now.co.uk/**

"Ward Cleaver's Prozac Fever"

Dads.com	**www.dads.com/**

Men's Health

The issues surrounding men's health are slightly different from those of women and so here are a few sites which look at men's very special needs.

Black Health Net	www.blackhealthnet.com/
Black Men's Health	www.blackmenshealth.org/
Dr. Koop's Community: Men's Health	www.drkoop.com/resource/mens
Gay Men's Health Crisis	www.gmhc.org/
Gay Men's Health Summit	www.temenos.net/summit/
Health Central	www.healthcentral.com/
Health Concerns Among Gay Men	www.thebody.com/sowadsky/gaymen.html
Health Library	www.healthlibrary.com/
Health Touch	www.healthtouch.com/
Impotence World Association	www.impotenceworld.org/
InteliHealth	www.intelihealth.com/
Male Health Center	www.malehealthcenter.com/
Men's Health	www.menshealth.com/
Men's Health – Clinique	www.clinique.com/mhealth.html
Men's Health – Keen.com	www.keen.com/
Men's Health – ThirdAge.com	www.thirdage.com/health/mens/
Men's Health Book Store	www.wellnessbooks.com/men/
Men's Health Consulting	www.menshealth.org/
Men's Health Network	www.menshealthnetwork.org/

Men's Health Online	www.mhealth.ru/
Men's Health Topics – Testicular Cancer	www.uro.com/tcancer.htm
MSN Men's Health	content.health.msn.com/
National Prostate Cancer Coalition	www.4npcc.org/
Prostate Health	www.prostatehealth.com/
Reuters Health Information	www.reutershealth.com/
Virtual Library – Men's Health Issues	www.vix.com/men/health/ health.html

Women's Health

The issues surrounding women's health are slightly different from those of men and so here are a few sites which look at women's very special needs.

Albyn Medical Practice	www.albyn-medical.co.uk/
All Cures	www.allhealth-info.com/
All Health	www.allhealth.com/womens/
BBC – Women's Health	www.bbc.co.uk/education/health/ womens/
BBC – Women's Health – STDs	www.bbc.co.uk/education/health/ womens/sexual.shtml
BUPA – Women's Health	www.bupa.co.uk/
Canadian Women's Health	www.cwhn.ca/indexfr.html
Cancer and Women's Health Links	www2.cybernex.net/~sune/ blinks.html

Cestria Health Centre	**members.aol.com/ChesterDoc/**
Feeding Question	**www.bbc.co.uk/education/health/ parenting/prfeed.shtml**
Fertility & Pregnancy Specialists	**www.fertilitytest.co.uk/**
Fibroids – Women's Health	**www.womens-health.co.uk/ fibroids.htm**
Fitness During Pregnancy	**www.childcare-now.co.uk/**
Health Square	**www.healthsquare.com/**
Healthy Women	**www.healthywomen.org/**
Jacobs Institute of Women's Health	**www.jiwh.org/**
Karen Lee's Virtual Clinic	**www.womencare.com/**
Medical Women's Federation	**www.m-w-f.demon.co.uk/**
National Asian Women's Health Organisation	**www.nawho.org/**
National Association of Professionals in Women's Health	**www.napwh.org/**

National Women's Health Information Center	**www.4woman.org/**

National Women's Health Organisation	www.gynpages.com/nwho
Natural & Alternative Approaches	www.healthy.net/womenshealth/
Pregnancy & Women's Health Information	www.womens-health.co.uk/
Society for Women's Health Research	www.womens-health.org/
The Mining Company: Women's Health	womenshealth.miningco.com/
Thrive Online	www.thriveonline.com/health/womensdoc/womensdoc.today.html
Vegetarian Pregnancy	www.vegsoc.org/Info/preg.html
WebMD: Women's Health	women.webmd.com/
Women's Health	www.womens-health.co.uk/
Women's Health	www.feminist.com/health.htm
Women's Health	www.womenshealth.com/
Women's Health Information Center	www.ama-assn.org/special/womh/womh.htm
Women's Health Interactive	www.womens-health.com/
Women's Health Net International	www.womenshealthnet.com/
Women's Health Resource Center	www.mayohealth.org/
Work & Pregnancy	www.babyworld.co.uk/information/working/work_pregnancy.htm

Hobbies

Kids of all ages, right up to 70 years and beyond, get a great deal of satisfaction from toys of all types. The Internet has websites from both the manufacturers and the enthusiasts.

Board Games

Many a winter's evening has been spent around a board game of some sort. Some of the most popular and enduring are...

Cluedo	www.cluedo.co.uk/
Fiendish Board Games	www.fbgames.co.uk/
Go	www.britgo.org/gopcres/gopcres1.html
Monopoly	www.monopoly.com/
Never Get Board!	uk.zone.msn.com/hub_board.asp
Risk	home.t-online.de/home/losmers/attila.htm
Scrabble	www.scrabble.com/
Sorry!	www.hasbro-interactive.com/
Trivial Pursuit	www.trivialpursuit.com/

Backgammon

This up-market ludo game has some very famous followers including Omar Sharif, I'm told.

Acey Ducey Backgammon	www.wingames.com/adback.html
Backgammon Deluxe	www.blackgames.net/bgammon.htm
FIBSJF	www.algonet.se/~svempa
Geert's Backgammon	huizen.dds.nl/~geertv
GNU Backgammon	www.gnu.org/software/gnubg/gnubg.html
JellyFish	effect.webbie.net/jelly.htm
MVP Backgammon	www.mvpsoft.com/soft-board.html
Netgammon	www.netgammon.com/
Pro Backgammon	www.wingames.com proback.html
Snowie 3	www.snowie3.com
Snowie Professional	www.oasya.com/

Chess

You need a particular way of thinking to master this game, and age doesn't seem to have much to do with it. There have been champions who are only just in their teens.

British Chess Federation	www.bcf.ndirect.co.uk/

| British Chess Magazine | www.bcmchess.co.uk/ |
| Chess Base | www.chessbase.com/ |

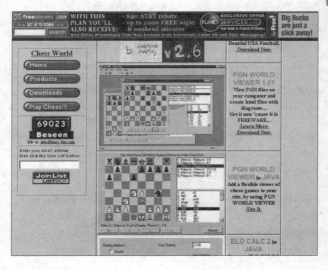

Chess World	chess.8m.com/
Garry Kasparov	www.clubkasparov.ru/
GNU Chess Web Interface	www.net-chess.com/gnu/
Interchess Email Chess	www.interchess.co.uk/
International Chess Federation	www.fide.com/
Internet Chess Club	www.chessclub.com/
London Chess Centre	www.chess.co.uk/

Mindscape	www.mindscape.com/
Rebel Decade	www.rebel.nl/index3.htm
Tasc Chess System	www.tasc.nl/

Draughts

Using the same board as Chess, Draughts (or Checkers as it is often referred to) is a great deal more straightforward to play.

Actual Checkers	www.atlantsoft.com
Checkers	www.magicwandsoft.com/ games/index.html
Checkers & Draughts	members.tripod.com/sgcheckers
Checkers Information	boardgamecentral.com/checkers/
Checkers Net Links	boardgames.about.com/ msub10.htm
Grooves Speed Team	www.angelfire.com/games/gst/
Online Checkers	www.pogo.com
Pond Checkers	www.pondcheckers.com/
Willow Creek Online	www.wcreekonline.com/

Card Games

I'm amazed at the number of games that can be played with a single pack of cards.

| Blackjack Depot | www.edepot.com/blackjack.html |
| Card Games Playable Over The Web | nxn.netgate.net/games2_XcardX .html |

Euchre	www.bright.net/~double/euchre.htm
Five by Five Poker	5x5poker.com/
House of Cards	thehouseofcards.com/online_games.html
Poker Races	PokerRaces.com/

Bridge

I was introduced to this game about 5 years ago and the interesting part about the game of Bridge is that the more you learn the more you realise you've got to learn.

Bridge – a fascinating card game!	www.math.auc.dk/~nwp/bridge
Bridge Lessons For Beginners	www.bridgeworld.com/begin.html
Bridge Today	www.bridgetoday.com/
Bridge World	www.bridgeworld.com/
Contract Bridge	netcafe.hypermart.net/bridge.html
Contract Bridge	www.uq.net.au/~zzjhardy/brmain.html
Contract Bridge Organisations	bridge.theriver.com/join.html
Easy Bridge	www.thegrid.net/shan/easybridge.htm
Learn To Play Bridge	www.acbl.org/notices/ltpb.stm
MSN Gaming Zone – Bridge	www.zone.com/asp/script/default.asp?game=brdg
PlayBridge	playbridge.com/

| Tutorial Bridge | learnbridge.com/ |
| World Bridge Federation | www.bridge.gr/ |

Patience (Solitaire)

If you're really bored, you can even play cards on your own.

Ace Solitaire	acegames.com/solitaire
Epsylon Games: Solitaires	www.games.taxxi.com/solit.html
Free 2 Play	www.homestead.com/free2play/solitaire.html
Gallery Solitaire	www.dplanet.ch/users/adrian.herzog/gallery
Grump Ventures.com	www.grumpventures.com/
Idiot's Delight	www.idiotsdelight.net/
PokerSquares.com	www.pokersquares.com/
PokSol	games.yadda.net/poksol
Solitaire Central	www.solitairecentral.com/
Tournament Games	www.tournamentgames.com/

Collections

Beanie Babies

Beanie Babies	www.a2zbeaniebabies.co.uk/
Beanie Babies	www.ty.com/
Beanie Babies Official Club	www.beaniebabyofficialclub.com/
Beanie Baby Bears	www.beaniebabiebears.co.uk/
Beanie Box UK	www.beanieboxuk.force9.co.uk/
Beanie Exchange	www.beanieexchange.net/

Beermats

Beer Collections	www.beercollections.com/
Beermat index	www.homestead.com/dunny2
Beermats	www.stormloader.com/olut/
Re: beermats	www.wasquare.com/forums/

China & Crystal

Collecting Wedgwood	www.suite101.com/article.cfm/ collecting_china/10729
Potteries, The	www.thepotteries.org/
Royal Doulton Collectables	www.broadband.co.uk/doulton/ messages/189.html
Waterford Crystal	www.waterford-usa.com/

Cigarette Cards

Card Collectables	www.cardcollectables.co.uk/

Cigarette and Tea cards	www.microscopy-uk.org.uk/mag/artaug98/mdcard.html
Cigarette Cards	www.cardking.bizhosting.com/
Cigarette Cards Central	www.cigcards.com/
English Cigarette Card Albums	www.the-forum.com/ephemera/engcc.htm
Framed Memories	www.cigarettecards.co.uk/
Pomeranian Cigarette cards	hometown.aol.com/soutra/pom1.htm
Tobacco Cards	www.tias.com/stores/arsh tobacco-cards-1.html
Wills cigarette cards	www.collectors.demon.co.uk/fccwills.html

Coins

Coin Dealers Directory	www.numis.co.uk/
Coin Link Numismatic Directory	www.coinlink.com/
Coin News	www.coin-news.com/
Coin Site	www.coinsite.com/
Coins of the UK	www.tclayton.demon.co.uk/coins.html
Collectors.com	www.coin-universe.com/
Cybercoins	www.nauticom.net/www/coins
Global Collector	www.globalcollector.ndirect.co.uk/
Interactive Collector	www.icollector.com/
Numismatica	www.limunltd.com/numismatica
Rare Coins	www.rare-coins.net/

| S & B Coins | www.users.globalnet.co.uk/~brcoin/ |
| Worldwide Coins | members.tripod.co.uk/worldwidecoins/ |

Matchboxes

Matchbox Collecting	www.ntnu.no/~dagfinnr/matchbox/matchbox.htm
Matchbox Label Collector	members.tripod.com/~hans_everink/titel.htm
Matchbox Labels	www.henry.demon.co.uk/mbox/mboxlabsindex.html
Virtual Matchbox Labels Collection	mkc.onego.ru/~stasdm/

Memorabilia

BeatleZone	www.beatlezone.com/
Classic Motorcycle Memorabilia	www.dropbears.com/c/classicmemories/
Cult TV Memorabilia	www.tv-memorabilia.demon.co.uk/links.htm
Grand Prix Memorabilia	www.gpm.cheltweb.co.uk/
Holly , Buddy – Memorabilia	www.geocities.com/SunsetStrip/Towers/5236/
Recollections	www.recollections.co.uk/

Phone Cards

| Global Collector | www.globalcollector.ndirect.co.uk/ |
| International Phone Card Exchange | www.ipce.com/ |

Phone Card Corner	www.angelfire.com/wy/cardcorner/
Swappers Phone Cards	www.geocities.com/Tokyo/Towers/1863/
World of Phone Cards	www.geocities.com/TheTropics/8370/

Stamps

American Philatelic Society	www.west.net/~stamps1/aps.html
Beginner's Guide to Stamp Collecting	alfin.computerworks.net/guide.htm
Crown Agents Stamp Bureau	www.casb.co.uk/
e-Stamp	www.e-stamp.com/
Global Collector	www.globalcollector.ndirect.co.uk/
Philatelic.com	www.philatelic.com/
Philately	www.philately.com/
Post Office	www.ukpo.com/
Stamp Link	www.stamplink.com/
Stamp Shows	www.stampshows.co.uk/
Wessex Philatelic Auctions	www.wessexphilatelic.com/

Trading Cards

Beckett Online	www.beckett.com/
Card Emporium	www.cardemporium.com/
Card Mall	www.cardmall.com/
First Base Trading Cards	www.narrows.com/firstbase/window.html-ssi
Fleer / Skybox Trading Cards	www.fleercorp.com/

Pokemon Trading Card Game	www.wizards.com/pokemon/
Pokemon World	www.pokemon.com/
SpaceMark Trading Cards	www.spacemark.com/
The World of Cards	www.cardcreations.ndirect.co.uk/
Trading Cards	www.wwcd.com/priceg/tcpg.html
Upper Deck Trading Cards	www.upperdeck.com/

Toys

These are toys for grown-ups. The kids won't get a look-in.

Aristo Craft Trains	www.aristocraft.com/
Classic Toys	www.classicengland.co.uk/ toysryou.htm
Matchbox	www.matchboxtoys.com/
TGV – Spotter's Guide	mercurio.iet.unipi.it/tgv/ spotter.html
Warhammer	www.games-workshop.co.uk/
Webville and Hypertext Railroad Company	www.spikesys.com/webville.html

Toy Manufacturers

Most of the major toy manufacturers have a website that gives details of their range of toys and, in some cases, gives you the opportunity to buy directly via the Internet.

| Barbie | www.barbie.com/ |
| Beanie Babies | www.ty.com/ |

| Brio | www.brio.co.uk/ |
| Corgi | www.corgi.co.uk/ |

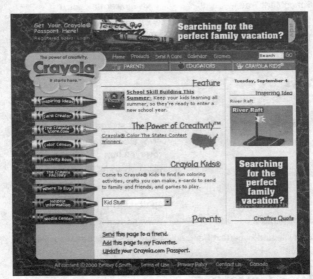

Crayola	www.crayola.com/
Fisher Price	www.fisher-price.com/
Goldsea Toys	www.goldseatoy-gift.com/
Handmaiden Gifts	www.handmaidengifts.com/
Hasbro Toys	www.hasbrotoys.com/home.html
Hornby	www.hornby.co.uk/

Kebrico	www.kebrico.ltd.uk/
K'NEX Central	www.knex.com/
Knex	www.knex.co.uk/
Koala Express	www.koalaexpress.com.au/
Learning Curve International	www.learningcurve.com/
Lego	www.lego.com/
LGB Railways	www.lgb.com/
Matchbox	www.matchboxtoys.com/
	www.matchbox.com/
Mattel	www.mattel.com/
Meccano	www.meccano.fr/
Micro Machines	www.micromachines.co.uk/
Middle-earth Toys	www.middleearthtoys.com/
Moose Toys	www.moosetoys.com/
Nintendo	www.nintendo.com/
Nintendo Gameboy	www.gameboy.com/
Playmobil	www.playmobil.de/
Pokemon	www.pokemon.com/
Quadro Toys	www.quadro-toys.co.uk/
Scalextric	www.scalextric.co.uk/
Schylling Toys	www.schylling.com/
Sega	www.sega.com/
Sega Dreamcast	www.dreamcast.com/
Sony	www.sony.com/
Sony Playstation	www.playstation.com/
Tomy	www.tomy.co.uk/

Toys of Wood   www.toys-of-wood.com/

Toy Suppliers

These sites are like toy shops in your living room (or wherever you happen to have your computer).

Ace Toy Company	www.toy.co.uk/
Active Toy Company	www.activetoy.co.uk/
Arcade Toy Shop	www.scoot.co.uk/ arcade_toy_shops/
Bannisters Matchbox & Toy Cars	www3.mistral.co.uk/trevorb/
Big Boys Toys	www.bigboystoyz.co.uk/
British Assoc. of Toy Retailers	www.batr.co.uk/
British Toy & Hobby Association	www.btha.co.uk/
Early Learning Centre	www.elc.co.uk/
Funstore	www.funstore.co.uk/acatalog/
Quadro Toys	www.quadro-toys.co.uk/
Toys 'R' Us	www.toysrus.co.uk/
Toyzone	www.toyzone.co.uk/

Jigsaw Puzzles

Whether it's collecting them, or making them, you'll find plenty of choice here. Some are 'real' jigsaws, others are online simulations. Just as much fun, but less chance of losing some of the pieces.

Animated Jigsaw Puzzles   clevermedia.com/arcade/jigsaw/ moving/

Artistic Wooden Jigsaw Puzzles	**www.newpuzzles.com/**
Biblical Jigsaw Puzzles	**www.hants.gov.uk/museum/ interact/index.html**
Boswandeling Jigsaw	**javaboutique.internet.com/ jsawpuzzle/**

Cartoon Jigsaws	**www.cwi.nl/~behr/Jigsaw/**
Chevron Jigsaw Puzzles	**www.chevroncars.com/play/ puzzle_demo/index.html**
Daily Jigsaw Puzzles	**clevermedia.com/arcade/jigsaw/**
Dallas Burn Java Puzzle	**www.burnsoccer.com/puzzle.html**
Free Jigsaw Puzzles.com	**freejigsawpuzzles.com/**
Java Jigsaws	**www.edbydesign.com/ scr_kids.html**
Jigsaw Jungle	**www.jigsawjungle.com/**
JigZone: Online Jigsaw Puzzles	**www.jigzone.com/**
Jixxa Jigsaw Puzzle	**www.risoftsystems.com/jixxa.asp**
justjigsaws.com	**www.justjigsaws.com/**

Logic Puzzle Page	www.halcyon.com/clifford/puzzle/index.htm
Meow Meow	www.scugog-net.com/room108/Puzzle/puzmeow.html
Morales Art Gallery	www.prints-r-us.com/puzzles/index.shtml
Puzzlemaker	www.puzzlemaker.com/
Puzzles Ink	www.puzzlesink.com/
Rodeo Rider	www.mcjeff.com/la/puzzle1.html

Stave Wooden Jigsaw Puzzles	www.stave.com/
TC's Jigsaw Puzzles	www.jigsaw-puzzles.co.uk/
Waving Duke Jigsaw	www.thinks.com/java/jigsaw/jigsaw.htm
Wentworth Wooden Jigsaw Club	www.wooden-jigsaws.com/
Wrebbit Jigsaw Puzzles	www.wrebbit.com/

Home

However humble, there's no place like home. Home is where most of us spend most of our lives and so it follows that homes will reflect the interests and maybe even the characteristics of the owner.

New Homes

Having lived in both new and old houses, there are advantages and disadvantages with both. You can't beat the character of older homes with unusual shaped rooms, interesting windows and high ceilings. Character, I suppose, is the word. But along with that character come draughts, high heating bills due to poor insulation and generally higher maintenance costs. New homes are thermally much more efficient and so heating is significantly reduced and with modern materials like uPVC, they are virtually maintenance free. But when describing the room, phrases about 'rabbit hutches' and 'swinging cats' frequently come to mind.

Antler Homes   **www.antlerhomes.co.uk/**
Ashwood Homes   **www.ashwoodhomes.co.uk/**

Banner Homes	www.banner-homes.co.uk/
Barratt Homes	www.ukpg.co.uk/barratt
Bryant Homes	www.bryant.co.uk/
David Wilson Homes	www.dwh.co.uk/
Laing	www.laing.co.uk/
McAlpine	www.alfred-mcalpine.co.uk/
Taylor Woodrow	www.taywood.co.uk/
Ward Homes	www.ward-homes.co.uk/
Wimpey Homes	www.wimpey.co.uk/

Property

I well remember trudging around scores of estate agents getting details of houses for sale. I also remember the postman bringing letters stuffed with property details. The Internet can reduce much of this because more and more estate agents are advertising on the Internet.

Brian & Linda Aaronson	www.realestatehelpline.com/
Bushells	www.bushells.com/
Chancellors	www.chancellors.co.uk/
CityLet	www.citylet.com/
Cluttons	www.cluttons.com/
Drivers Jonas	www.djonas.co.uk/
Easier	www.easier.co.uk/
Egerton	www.egertonproperty.co.uk/
Euro Properties	www.europropertynet.com/

Fraser Beach	www.select-e.com/
Friend & Falcke	www.friendandfalcke.co.uk/
Hamptons	www.hamptons.co.uk/
HomeCheck	www.homecheck.co.uk/
Janice Leverington	www.noplacelikehome.com/
Jeannette Hutchison	www.conejohomes.com/
Jim Hanrahan	www.sarasota-properties.com/

| John D Wood | www.johndwood.co.uk/ |

Judy McCutchin	www.dallashomes.com/
King Sturge	www.kingsturge.co.uk/
Knight Frank	www.knightfrank.co.uk/
Linda Soesbe	www.coloradohomesource.com/
Lisa DeNardo	www.yourhomeplace.com/
London Home Net	www.londonhomenet.com/
Mary Calvert	www.marycalvert.com/
Move	www.move.co.uk/
Nell Shukes	www.nellshukes.com/
Nigel Wain	www.uniquerealestate.com/
Nora Ling-Lane	www.noralane.com/
Property 4 U	www.aproperty4u.com/
Property Broker	www.propertybroker.co.uk/
Property Finder	www.propertyfinder.co.uk/
Property Shop	www.e-propertyshop.com/
Realtor	www.realtor.com/
Right Move	www.rightmove.co.uk/
Ron Resnick	www.teamloudoun.com/
Russ Harrist	www.realtyshop.net/
Strettons	www.strettons.co.uk/
Strutt & Parker	www.struttandparker.co.uk/
Terry Yapp	www.terryyapp.com
Thomas & Sally Cook	www.torontorealestate.ca/
UK Property Shop	www.ukpropertyshop.co.uk/
Under One Roof	www.underoneroof.co.uk/

Uswitch	www.uswitch.com/
Winkworth	www.winkworth.co.uk/
Wynne Achatz	www.wynnea.com/

Removals

Moving home ranks alongside bereavement and divorce in the Top 10 list of stress-inducing activities. At least get a good company to move the contents from your old home to your new home.

| Interpak | www.interpak.co.uk/ |
| Moves | www.moves.co.uk/ |

| Pickfords | www.pickfords.co.uk/ |

DIY

Doing the job yourself can save a great deal of money. On the other hand it can cost you a great deal if you don't do it properly. Be sure you know what you're doing before embarking on major renovations to your home.

B&Q	www.diy.com/
Black & Decker	www.blackanddecker.com/
Bostik	www.bostik.com/
Cookson's Tools	www.cooksons.com/
Draper Tools	www.draper.co.uk/
Dulux Paints	www.dulux.com/
Homebase	www.homebase.co.uk/
Jewson	www.jewson.co.uk/
Quickgrip	www.quickgrip.com/
Screwfix	www.screwfix.com/
Stanley Tools	www.stanleyworks.com/
Wickes	www.wickes.com/

Electrical Goods

The modern home is a highly mechanised environment which takes away much of the drudgery and consequently gives us more time to spend with each other.

Best Stuff	www.beststuff.co.uk/
Comet	www.comet.co.uk/

Dixons	www.dixons.co.uk/
Firebox	www.firebox.com/
Helpful Home Shopping Co	www.helpful.co.uk/
iQVC	www.iqvc.com/
Powerhouse	www.powerhouse-online.co.uk/
QVC UK	www.qvcuk.com/
Remote controls	www.remotecontrols.co.uk/
Tempo	www.tempo.co.uk/
Unbeatable	www.unbeatable.co.uk/
Value Direct	www.value-direct.co.uk/
Web Electricals	www.webelectricals.co.uk/

Furniture

You need something to sit on, to eat from and something to sleep in. You'll also need other sundry items like cabinets to store or display all the silver and crystal you've accumulated over the years or received as wedding gifts.

Almara	www.almahome.co.uk/
Benns	www.benns-furniture.co.uk/
Blue Deco	www.craftdesign-london.com/
British Furniture Manufacturers	www.bfm.org.uk/
Brown's Furniture Company	www.browns-furniture.co.uk/
Cash-save Cane Furniture	www.cane-furniture.co.uk/
Country Desks	www.countrydesks.co.uk/
Courts plc	www.courtsretail.com/

Dimension Manufacturing	www.scoot.co.uk/dimension_manufacturing/
Dovetail Furniture	www.dovetail-furniture.co.uk/
Elite Leisure Furniture	www.elite-leisure-furniture.co.uk/
Ercol Furniture	www.ercol-furniture.com/
Found	www.foundat.co.uk/
Furniture & Fittings Directory	www.fmd.co.uk/cat/furniture/
Furniture Directory	www.furniture.org.uk/
Furniture, Interiors and Gardens	www.fig.co.uk/
Furniture Network	www.furniturenet.co.uk/
Furniture online	www.furniture-on-line.co.uk/
FurnitureFind.com	www.furniturefind.com/
Futon Direct	www.futondirect.co.uk/
Habitat	www.habitat.net/
IKEA	www.ikea.co.uk/
Interior Internet	www.interiorinternet.com/
Iron Bed Company	www.ironbed.co.uk/
JPA Furniture	www.jpa-furniture.com/
Knightsbridge Furniture	www.knightsbridge-furniture.co.uk/
Lutyens Design Associates	www.lutyens-furniture.com/
Magnet	www.magnet.co.uk/
McCord	www.mccord.uk.com/
Metal Maniacs	www.wrought-iron-furniture.com/
MFI Homeworks	www.mfi.co.uk/mfihomeworks/
Oakridge	www.oakridgedirect.co.uk/

Ocean	www.oceancatalogue.co.uk/
Osborne Furniture	www.osbornefurniture.com/
Oxford Furniture Warehouse	www.oxford-furniture.co.uk/
Quinn Furniture Ltd	www.quinn-furniture.co.uk/
Robert Winchurch Furniture	www.winchurch-furniture.co.uk/

Sofa Beds	www.sofabeds.co.uk/
Sofas Direct	www.classicchoice.co.uk/
Stocker Furniture	www.stocker-furniture.co.uk/
Stompa	www.stompa.co.uk/
Thistle Joinery	www.thistlejoinery.co.uk/
Tim Wood Furniture	www.timwoodfurniture.co.uk/
Treske Solid Wood Furniture	www.yorkshirenet.co.uk/treske/
Virtual Cane UK	cane-rattan-furniture.co.uk/
Wade Furniture	www.webswonder.co.uk/wade/
Websters Distinctive Furniture	www.websters-furniture.co.uk/
Wharfside Furniture	www.wharfside-furniture.co.uk/
Whitemeadow Upholstery	www.whitemeadow-furniture.co.uk/
Woodberry Brothers & Haines	www.woodberry-furniture.com/
Wrenn Furniture	www.wrenn-furniture.co.uk/

Garden

I do like a well-maintained garden. Unfortunately I don't like doing the maintenance. If you do, visit some of these sites.

British Gardening Online	www.oxalis.co.uk/
Crocus	www.crocus.co.uk/
eSeeds.com	www.eseeds.com/
Exhibition Seeds	www.exhibition-seeds.co.uk/
Garden.com	www.garden.com/
Garden Shop	www.thegardenshop.co.uk/
Garden World	www.gardenworld.co.uk/
International Bulb Society	www.bulbsociety.com/
Nicky's Nursery	www.nickys-nursery.co.uk/seeds
Pelco	www.pelcogarden.com/
Shrubs Direct	www.shrubsdirect.com/
Woolmans	www.woolmans.co.uk/

Insurance

We hope we'll never need it, but if the unthinkable should happen, you should be covered. Never insure for less than the full cost of rebuilding plus the new price of all contents.

A1 Insurance	www.a1insurance.co.uk/
ABBA Home Insurance Direct	members.aol.com/mattcalton/ index2.htm
Birmingham Midshires Financial Services	www.birmingham-midshires .co.uk/

CGU	www.cgudirect.co.uk/
Churchill Insurance	www.churchill.co.uk/
Clover Insurance Home Insurance	www.clover-insurance.demon.co.uk/household.htm
Cornhill	www.cornhill.co.uk/
Direct Line	www.directline.co.uk/
Eagle Star Direct	www.eaglestardirect.co.uk/
Edinburgh Solicitors Property	www.espc.co.uk/
Express Insurance Group	www.expressinsurancegroup.co.uk/
Fernet Insurance Brokers Ltd	www.fernet.com/uk/
Home Insurance	www.landg.com/homeins/homeins1.html
HomeLine Direct	www.insurance-line.co.uk/main.htm
Home-Net UK	www.midway.co.uk/insurance/home
HomeQuote Insurance UK	home.quote.co.uk/
Legal & General UK	www.legal-and-general.co.uk/
Merlin Insurance Consultants	www.merlins.demon.co.uk/insurance/
MoneyNet	www.moneynet.ltd.uk/
Nationwide Finance	www.nwide.freeserve.co.uk/
Net Insurance Services	www.nis.ndirect.co.uk/
Rapid Care Insurance	www.domgen.com/
Reallymoving.com	www.reallymoving.com/
Royal & Sun Alliance Insurance	www.royal-and-sunalliance.com/

SoreEyes – Insurance Quotes   www.soreeyes.co.uk/
Woolwich Insurance Services   www.woolwich.co.uk/

Interior Design

To make your house the envy of your friends, you'll need to think about the design of the interior. But interior design will also help you get the most from the available space.

Abiaz	www.abiaz.com/
Cavendish Interiors	www.cavendishinteriors.co.uk/
Click Deco	www.clickdeco.com/
Cross Interiors	www.crossinteriors.com/
Designed Interiors	www.designedinteriors.com/
Eclectic Interiors	www.eclecticinteriors.com/
French Interiors	www.frenchinteriors.com/
Home Interiors	www.homeinteriors.co.uk/
Home Portfolio	www.homeportfolio.com/
Ikea	www.ikea.com/
Integrated Interiors	www.integratedinteriors.com/
Interior Design & Decoration	www.iddv.com/
Interior Internet	www.interiorinternet.com/
Matchroom	www.matchroom.demon.co.uk/
My Interior Decorator	www.myinteriordecorator.com/
Old House Interiors	www.oldhouseinteriors.com/
Style Craft Interiors	www.stylecraftinteriors.com/

Terence Conran	www.conran.co.uk/
Village Interiors	www.villageinteriors.com/

Knick-Knacks

It's the little knick-knacks that really give the home the character of the occupant. These websites, by and large, sell lots of things you'd like, but not a lot you actually need.

Appeal	www.appeal-blinds.co.uk/
Argos Online	www.argos.co.uk/
Battle Orders	www.battleorders.co.uk/
Bottle Rack, The	www.thebottlerack.com/
Carpet Right	www.carpetright.co.uk/
Chadder & Co	www.chadder.com/
Chesney's	www.antiquefireplace.co.uk/
CP Hart	www.cphart.co.uk/
Dyson	www.dyson.com/
eShop	www.eshop.co.nz/
Flames	flames.estreet.co.uk/
Habitat	www.habitat.co.uk/
Hillarys	www.hillarys.co.uk/
Holding Company, The	www.theholdingcompany.co.uk/
Home Zone	www.shoppersuniverse.com/
House Mail Order	www.housemailorder.co.uk/
Index Online	www.indexshop.com/
Innovations	www.innovations.co.uk/

Liberty	www.liberty-of-london.com/
Maelstrom	www.maelstrom.co.uk/
Marks & Spencer	www.marks-and-spencer.co.uk/
Mathmos	www.mathmos.co.uk/
Mr Resistor	www.mr-resistor.co.uk/
Nauticalia	www.nauticalia.co.uk/
Plümo	www.plumo.com/
Rabid Home	www.rabidhome.com/
South Downs Trading Company	www.southdowns.co.uk/
Sträad Direct	www.straad.co.uk/
Tie Rack	www.tierack.com/
West of England Reproduction Furniture	www.reproductionfurniture.com/

Kitchen Accessories

The kitchen is often described as the centre of a house. There are lots of gadgets you need and even more you'd like available from websites the world over.

All-Clad Online	www.metrokitchen.com/
Appliance Online	www.applianceonline.co.uk/
Be-Direct	www.be-direct.co.uk/
Brabantia	www.brabantia.com/
Chef's Store	www.chefs-store.com/
Cook Craft	www.cookcraft.com/
Cooks Kitchen	www.kitchenware.co.uk/

Cucina Direct	www.cucinadirect.co.uk/
Divertimenti	www.divertimenti.co.uk/
Empire Direct	www.empiredirect.co.uk/
Home Creations	www.myinternet.co.uk/home
Home Electrical Direct	www.hed.co.uk/
Internet Cookshop	www.scottsargeant.com/
Kitchenware	www.kitchenware.co.uk/
Le Creuset	www.lecreuset.com/
Magnet	www.magnet.co.uk/
Pots and Pans	www.pots-and-pans.co.uk/
Russell Hobbs	www.russell-hobbs.com/
Small Island Trader	www.smallislandtrader.com/
Tefal	www.tefal.co.uk/

Whitegoods

Whitegoods are generally found in the kitchen or laundry room. The manufacturers are quick to advertise their products on the Internet.

AEG	www.aeg-direct.com/
Aga & Rayburn	www.aga-rayburn.co.uk/
Belling	www.belling.co.uk/
Bosch	www.bosch-direct.com/
Creda	www.creda.co.uk/
Electrolux	www.electrolux.co.uk/
Hoover	www.hoover.co.uk/

Hotpoint	www.hotpoint.co.uk/
Miele	www.miele.co.uk/
Neff	www.neff.co.uk/
Panasonic	www.panasonic.co.uk/
Philips	www.philips.co.uk/
Smeg	www.smeguk.com/
Stoves	www.stoves.co.uk/
Whirlpool	www.whirlpool.co.uk/

Zanussi	www.zanussi.com/

Utilities

It's the stuff that's pumped into our homes that seems to generate bills of ever-increasing size. This will be familiar to parents of teenagers who leave taps running, leave lights on, leave the cooker on and then go for a 2 hour chat on the phone.

Gas/Electricity

Aquila Energy	www.aquilaenergy.com/uk/
British Gas	www.britishgas.com/
Electricity Direct	www.electricity-direct.com/

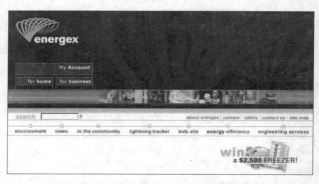

Energex	www.energex.com.au/
energyOn.co.uk	www.energyon.co.uk/
Great Southern Energy	www.gsenergy.com.au/
Npower	www.npower.com/
NY State Electric & Gas	www.nyseg.com/
Ofgem	www.ofgem.gov.uk/
Power Brokers	www.thepowerbrokers.co.uk/
Powergen	www.pgen.com/

Puget Sound Energy	www.pse.com/
Scottish Power	www.scottishpower.co.uk/
Seeboard plc	www.seeboard.com/
UK Power	www.ukpower.co.uk/

Telephone Companies

ABS Telecom	www.abstelecom.com/
AT&T	www.att.com/
British Telecommunications	www.bt.com/
Cable & Wireless	www.cw.com/
Eckoh	www.eckoh.com/
Eurotel	www.eurotel.co.uk/
Excel Communications	www.excel.com/
NTL	www.ntl.com/
Oftel	www.oftel.gov.uk/
Phone Tips	www.advantagegroup.co.uk/
Quip	www.quip.co.uk/

Water

Anglian Water Services Ltd	www.anglianwater.co.uk/
Bournemouth & West Hampshire Water plc	www.bwhwater.co.uk/
Bristol Water plc	www.bristolwater.co.uk/
Cambridge Water	www.cambridge-water.co.uk/
Colorado Springs Utilities	www.csu.org/water/res_water.html
Crystal Spring	www.crystalspring.co.uk/

Drinking Water	www.official-documents.co.uk/document/doe/drinking/sumcont.htm
Dwr Cymru Cyfyngedig	www.hyder.com/

Essex & Suffolk Water	www.eswater.co.uk/
Florence Water Treatment	www.flo-utilities.com/water/water_treatment.htm
Garland – Water Utilities Dept	www.ci.garland.tx.us/water/cogwtitl.htm
Lubbock – Water Utilities	water.ci.lubbock.tx.us/
Mid Kent Water plc	www.midkent.co.uk/
Northumbrian Water Ltd	www.nwl.co.uk/
Ofwat	www.ofwat.gov.uk/
Portsmouth Water plc	www.portsmouthwater.co.uk/

Severn Trent Water Ltd	**www.stwater.co.uk/**
South East Water plc	**www.southeastwater.co.uk/**
Southern Water Services Ltd	**www.southernwater.co.uk/**
South Staffordshire Water	**www.south-staffordshire.com/**
South West Water Ltd	**www.south-west-water.co.uk/**
Sutton And East Surrey Water plc	**www.waterplc.com/**
Tendring Hundred Water Services Ltd	**www.thws.co.uk/**
Thames Water Utilities Ltd	**www.thames-water.com/**
Three Valleys Water plc	**www.3valleys.co.uk/**
United Utilities	**www.unitedutilities.com/**
Wessex Water Services Ltd	**www.wessexwater.co.uk/**
Yorkshire Water Services Ltd	**www.yorkshirewater.com/**

Lifestyle

The term 'lifestyle' seems to cover a multitude of sins. Perhaps 'miscellaneous' might be more appropriate.

Astrology

Can it really be that one-twelfth of the world's population have the same future that I have? If you want to know what fortune has in hand for your one-twelfth, check out some of these sites.

Aquarian Age	www.aquarianage.org/
Asian Astrology	www.jadegate.com/astro
Astro Atlas	www.astro.ch/atlas
Astrola's Metaphysical Den	www.astrola.com/
Astrological Association of Great Britain	www.astrologer.com/
Astrological Horoscopes & Forecasts	www.astro-horoscopes.com/
Astrology	www.canoe.ca/Fun/home.html
Astrology A to Z	www.astrologer.com/websites/astrol.html

Astrology Et Al	www.astrologyetal.com/
Astrology Matrix	www.thenewage.com/
Astrology Online	www.astrology-online.com/
Astrology World	www.astrology-world.com/
Daily Humorscope	www.humorscope.com/
Horary Astrology	www.horary.com/
Horoscopes from Russell Grant	www.russellgrant.com/
Jon Sandifer	www.jonsandifer.com/
Jonathan Cainer	stars.metawire.com/
Kozmik Horoscopes	www.demon.co.uk/kdm/hscope1.html
Love Astrology	love.astrology.net/
Matrix Astrology Software	www.astral.demon.co.uk/
Metalog Astrology	www.astrologer.com/
MSN Web Communities: Astrology	communities.msn.com/astrology
Netstrology: Daily Horoscopes	www.techweb.com/horoscope
Rob Brezsny's Real Astrology	www.realastrology.com/
Starlight Astrology	www.starlightastrology.com/
Sunrise Magazine	www.sunrisemag.com/
What's in Your Stars	www.msn.co.uk/page/8-150.asp
Women.Astrology.net	women.astrology.net/
Your Daily Horoscope	www.4yourhoroscope.com/
Your Daily Horoscope	www.astrocom.com/

Dating

Computer dating is not new, but Internet computer dating is. You enter your details, pay the fee and with luck you'll be matched to your perfect partner.

1-2-1 Internet Dating Agency	www.aquiesce.co.uk/1-2-1/index2.htm
ABC UK Dating & Personals	www.abcdating.co.uk/
Absolute Match	www.absolutematch.com/
American Singles	www.americansingles.com/
Classical Partners	www.classicalpartners.co.uk/
Computer Dating	www.computer-dating.com/
Cupid's Network	www.cupidnet.com/
Date.com	www.date.com/
Dateable	www.dateable.com/
Dating Club	www.datingclub.com/
Dating Direct	www.datingdirect.co.uk/
Dating Direct	www.datingdirect.com/
Dating.com	www.dating.com/
For Singles	www.forsingles.com/
Free Dating Agency	www.geocities.com/southbeach/strand/2142
Free UK Dating Agency	www.lovefinder.co.uk/
Friendfinder	www.friendfinder.com/
Gay Dating UK	www.gay-dating.co.uk/dating/indexj.html

Justmates	www.justmates.com/
Kiss.com	www.kiss.com/
London Dating	www.londondating.co.uk/
Love Agency	www.loveagency.com/
Love City	www.lovecity.com/
Loving You	www.lovingyou.com/
Match.com	www.match.com/
Matchmaker.com	www.matchmaker.com/
On Match	www.onmatch.com/
One & Only	www.one-and-only.com/
Online Encounters	www.online-encounters.com/
Other Singles	www.othersingles.com/
Pairs	www.pairs.com/
People 2 People	www.people2people.com/
Romancero.com	www.romancero.com/
RSVP	www.rsvp.com.au/
Search Partner	www.searchpartner.com/
Singles.com	www.singles.com/
Soulmates	www.soulmates.com.au/
The Kiss	www.thekiss.com/
Two's Company Dating Service	www.twoscompany.co.uk/
Venus Dating UK	www.venusdating.co.uk/
Victoria's Agency	www.victoriasagency.com/

Internet Chat

If you're feeling lonely, you can have a chat with someone else, or several others, across the Internet. You will probably find that the person you're speaking to is from another part of the world. Some of the chatlines have specific themes so if you use them, you should stick to the designated topics.

Catholicity	www.catholicity.com/
Chat Box	www.chatbox.com/
Chat City	www.chatcity.com.au/
Chat Freak	www.chatfreak.com/
Chat Shack	www.chatshack.net/
Chat Town	www.chattown.com/
Chat Web	www.chatweb.net/
Christian Cafe	www.christiancafe.com/
Hearme.com	www.hearme.com/
Hyperchat	www.hyperchat.com/
ICQ	www.icq.net/
Internet Relay Chat	www.irchelp.org/
Keep Talking	www.keeptalking.com/
L'Hotel Chat	www.hotelchat.com/
OmniChat!	www.4-lane.com/
Parachat	www.parachat.com/
PeopleLink	www.peoplelink.com/
Quickchat	www.quickchat.org/
Teenchat	www.teenchat.co.uk/

UKchat	www.ukchat.com/
Womenchat	www.womenchat.com/
Yahoo! Chat	chat.yahoo.com/

Religion

Information about all of the world's religions can be found on the Internet. These are but a few.

About Islam and Muslims	www.unn.ac.uk/societies/islamic/
Alternative Religions	altreligion.about.com/
Basics Of Sikhi	www.sikhi.demon.co.uk/
Belief Net	www.beliefnet.com/
Biblealive	www.internet-uk.com/bible-a
British Humanist Association	www.humanism.org.uk/
British Religion and Philosophy	www.stg.brown.edu/projects/ hypertext/landow/victorian/ religion/philtl.html
Buddhism & Meditation books	www.tharpa.com/
Calendar of Religious Festivals	www.namss.org.uk/fests.htm
Catholic Encyclopedia	www.knight.org/advent/cathen/ cathen.htm
Catholic Online On The Web	www.catholic.org/
Christian Faith Groups	www.religioustolerance.org/ var_rel.htm
Finding God in Cyberspace	www.fontbonne.edu/libserv/fgic/ intro.htm
Hinduism online	www.himalayanacademy.com/

Investigating Islam	www.islamic.org.uk/
Islamic City	www.islam.org/
Islamic Research Academy	www.stir.ac.uk/relstd/afa/ jerusalem/welcome.htm
Jewish Museum, London	www.ort.org/communit/ jewmusm/home.htm
Muslim Directory	www.muslimdirectory.co.uk/ newpages/autext.html
Muslim Prayer Times	salam.muslimsonline.com/
Mysticism in World Religions	www.digiserve.com/mystic/
New Religious Movements	cti.itc.virginia.edu/~jkh8x/ soc257/profiles.html
Quakers	www.quaker.org.uk/
Religion	www.hbuk.co.uk/ap/journals/rl/
Religion in Everyday Life	news.mpr.org/features/199804/ 06_newsroom_religion/
Religion Links	www.gty.org/~phil/bookmark.htm
Religion on the Web	users.ox.ac.uk/~worc0337/ serious/religion.html
Religions and Religious Studies	www.clas.ufl.edu/users/gthursby/ rel/
Religious Education Exchange	re-xs.ucsm.ac.uk/
Religious Studies - Africa	www.sas.upenn.edu/ African_Studies/About_African/ ww_relig.html
Sikh Museum	www.sikhmuseum.org/
Totally Jewish	www.totallyjewish.com/

Virtual Religion Index	religion.rutgers.edu/vri/
Watchman Index of Cults and Religions	www.watchman.org/indxmenu.htm
Western Religions	www.mrdowling.com/605westr.html

Men

These sites will be of particular interest to men, although there is a great deal here for everyone.

A Man's Life	www.manslife.com/
Atlanta Reproductive Health Centre	www.ivf.com/
Bi.org	bi.org/
Clinique – For Men Only	www.clinique.com/
FitnessOnline	www.fitnessonline.com/
GMHC: HIV and AIDS Information	www.gmhc.org/
Health Magazines – Healthy Living	www3.healthgate.com/
Holistic Health Plus – Hair Color	www.holistichealthplus.com/
LookSmart Live!	live.looksmart.com/
Manhood Online	www.manhood.com.au/
Men's Fitness Online	www.mensfitness.com/
Men's Journal	www.mensjournal.com/
Muscle and Fitness Online	www.muscle-fitness.com/
Nutrition For You	www.nutrition4you.com/
OnHealth Columns	www.onhealth.com/ch1/

Peak Conditioning	www.peakconditioning.com/
Phish – Phunky Bitches	www.phunky.com/
Pola Cosmetics	www.pola.com/
Sex: A Man's Guide	www.sexamansguide.com/
Smack 'em Yack 'em	www.smackem.com/
Welcome to the Vita-Men!	www.vita-men.com/
YMCA	www.ymca.net/

Women

It has finally been recognised that this is the largest untapped market on the Internet. These sites are aimed specifically at women.

Beme.com	www.beme.com/
British Women Pilots' Association	www.bwpa.demon.co.uk/
British Women Racing Drivers Club	www.autolinkuk.co.uk/
Cabinet Office – Women's Unit	www.womens-unit.gov.uk/
Charlotte Street	www.charlottestreet.com/
Engender	www.engender.org.uk/
Femail.co.uk	www.femail.co.uk/
Feminist Archive	www.femarch.mcmail.com/
Freedom UK	www.freedom.co.uk/
Handbag.com	www.handbag.com/
iCircle	www.icircle.com/
Int'l Council of Jewish Women	www.icjw.org.uk/

Internet UK Gay Guides	www.gayguide.co.uk/
iVillage	ivillage.co.uk/
Kids & a Career	www.bbc.co.uk/education/having/index.shtml
Life UK	www.lifeuk.org/
Medical Women's Federation	www.m-w-f.demon.co.uk/
Ministers for Women	www.open.gov.uk/womens-unit/
National Federation of Women's Institutes	www.nfwi.org.uk/
National Women's Council of Ireland	www.nwci.ie/
National Women's Register	www.nwr.org/
Network of East–West Women	www.neww.org./
New Woman	www.newwoman.co.uk
Planet Girl	www.planetgrrl.com/
Scottish Women's History Network	swhn.gcal.ac.uk/
The Women's Room	www.msn.co.uk/womens/
WNAS	www.wnas.org.uk/
Woman's Hour	www.bbc.co.uk/radio4/womanshour/
Women in Publishing	www.cyberiacafe.net/wip/
Women Welcome Women	www.womenwelcomewomen.org.uk/
Women.com	www.women.com/
Women's History Review	www.triangle.co.uk/whr/

Women's National Commission	www.thewnc.org.uk/
Women's Press	www.the-womens-press.com/
Women's Resource Centre	www.wrc.uninet.co.uk/
Women's Royal Voluntary Service	members.tripod.com/~wrvs/
Women's Unit	www.womens-unit.gov.uk/
Working Girls	communities.msn.co.uk/ forwomen

Kids

Amazon Kids	www.amazonkids.co.uk/
ArgoSphere	www.argosphere.net/
Children's BBC	www.bbc.co.uk/cbbc/
Disney Channel	disney.go.com/disneychannel/
F9 Kids	kids.f9.net.uk/
Fox Kids	www.foxkids.co.uk/
Kids Channel	www.kids-channel.co.uk/
Kids Domain UK	www.kidsdomain.co.uk/
Kids Fun for All Ages	www.kidsfun.co.uk/
Kids on the Web	www.brookes.ac.uk/rms/ kidsontheweb/
Kids Organic Club	www.kids.organics.org/
Toyzone	www.toyzone.co.uk/

| Yahooligans | www.yahooligans.com/ |

Teenagers

Birth Control & Contraception for Teenagers	www.avert.org/cpills.htm
Digital Teen Chat	www.teen-chat.net/
Get Together Online	communities.msn.co.uk/people
Habbo Hotel	www.habbo.com/
Mind, Body & Soul	www.mindbodysoul.gov.uk/
mykindaplace.com	www.mykindaplace.com/
Pupiline	www.pupiline.net/
So – BBC Online	www.bbc.co.uk/so/
Surviving Adolescence	www.rcpsych.ac.uk/info/help/adol/index.htm
Talking Teenagers	www.bbc.co.uk/radio2/inside/campaigns/teens_home.shtml
TeenChat	www.teenchat.co.uk/
Teen Today	www.teentoday.co.uk/
The Junction	www.thej.net/
Trouble	www.trouble.co.uk/
Youth 2 Youth	www.youth2youth.co.uk/

Silver Surfers

There is a marked increase in the number of retired people who are digging into their savings to buy a PC. Good luck to them.

Gordon, Guy – Silver Surfer	www.3gcs.com/silver_surfer/
Hells Geriatrics.com	www.hellsgeriatrics.com/

koolsilver.com	www.koolsilver.com/
Silver Links	ourworld.compuserve.com/ homepages/smilne6/silv.htm
Silver Surfers Main Index	www.silversurfers.uk.com/
Silver Surfers	www.silversurfers.tv/
Silver Surfers Web Asylum	www.silversurfer.freeserve.co.uk/
Silver-Surfers	www.silver-surfers.uk.com/sites/ silversurfers/index2.html
SilverSurfersClub.com	www.silversurfersclub.com/
SilverSurfers UK	www.silversurfers.net/
Technomum	www.technomum.co.uk/

Lesbian & Gay

It's important, in a book like this, to cover all aspects of life. If you think you might be offended by the contents of some of these websites, don't go there.

Coming Out and Staying Out	www.gmhp.demon.co.uk/coming- out/
Freedom UK	www.freedomuk.com/
Gay Agenda	www.gayagenda.com/
Gay-Lesbian Issues	gaylesissues.about.com/
Gay and Lesbian Politics	www.indiana.edu/~glbtpol/
Gay & Lesbian Task Force	www.ngltf.org/
Gay Times and Diva	www.gaytimes.co.uk/
Gay.uk.net	www.gay.uk.net/
GaytoZ	www.gaytoz.com/

Internet UK Gay Guides	www.gayguide.co.uk/
Lesbian Life	lesbianlife.about.com/
Lesbian.org	www.lesbian.org/
Lesbian & Gay Switchboard	www.llgs.org.uk/
National Center for Lesbian Rights	www.nclrights.org/index.html
Outcast Magazine	www.outcastmagazine.co.uk/
OutProud!	www.outproud.org/
Parents, Families and Friends of Lesbians and Gays	www.pflag.org/
Queer Nation	www.cs.cmu.edu/Web/People/ mjw/Queer/MainPage.html
QX Magazine	www.qxmag.co.uk/

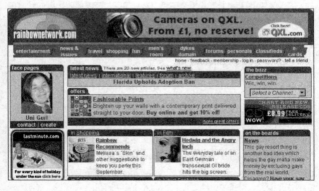

Rainbow Network	www.rainbownetwork.com/

Motoring

I'm sure some people must have been born with petrol in their veins. Motor cars and bikes are the love of some people's lives. For others, they are merely a means of getting from a to b.

Auto Manufacturers

All of the major motor manufacturers have a website which in most cases is their catalogue in a slightly different form. There are, however, some surprises in store on some of the sites.

AC	**www.accars.com/**
Alfa Romeo	**www.alfaromeo.com/**
Aston Martin	**www.astonmartin.com/**
Audi	**www.audi.com/**
Bentley	**www.rolls-royceandbentley.co.uk/**
BMW	**www.bmw.com/**
Bristol	**www.bristolcars.co.uk/**
Cadillac	**www.cadillac.com/**
Caterham	**www.caterham.co.uk/**
Chevrolet	**www.chevrolet.com/**

Auto Manufacturers

Chrysler	www.chryslerjeep.co.uk/
Citroen	www.citroen.com/
Daewoo	www.dm.co.kr/
Ferrari	www.ferrari.it/
Fiat	www.fiat.com/
Ford	www.ford.com/
Holden	www.hsv.com.au/
Honda	www.honda.com/
Hyundai	www.hyundai-car.co.uk/
Isuzu	www.isuzu.com/
Jaguar	www.jaguar.com/
Jeep	www.chryslerjeep.co.uk/
Kia	www.kia.com/
Land Rover	www.landrover.com/
Lexus	www.lexus.com/
Lotus	www.lotuscars.co.uk/
Marcos	www.marcos.co.uk/
Maserati	www.maserati.it/
Mazda	www.mazda.co.uk/
Mercedes Benz	www.mercedes-benz.com/
MG	www.mgcars.com/
Mini	www.mini.com/
Mitsubishi	www.mitsubishi-cars.co.uk/
Morgan	www.morgan-motor.co.uk/
Nissan	www.nissan-usa.com/

Opel	www.opel.com/
Peugeot	www.peugeot.com/
Porsche	www.porsche.com/
Proton	www.proton.co.uk/
Renault	www.renault.com/
Rolls Royce	www.rolls-royceandbentley.co.uk/
Rover	www.rovercars.com/
Saab	www.saab.com/
SEAT	www.seat.com/

ŠkodaAuto

Showroom
World
Forum
Company
Motorsport

Company:
Look through the official
reports, history, environmental
policy, and further more.

World:
Find the way to the Skoda
partners world-wide.

Showroom:
Skoda cars are here to enrich
your life.

© SkodaAuto

Skoda	www.skoda-auto.com/
Subaru	www.subaru.com/
Suzuki	www.suzuki.co.uk/
Toyota	www.toyota.co.uk/

TVR	www.tvr-eng.co.uk/
Vauxhall	www.vauxhall.co.uk/
Volkswagen	www.vw.com/
Volvo	www.car.volvo.se/

Bike Manufacturers

Like cars, manufacturers of bikes also have their sites on the Internet.

BMW	www.bmw.com/
Ducati	www.ducati.com/
Harley Davidson	www.harley-davidson.com/
Honda	www.honda.com/
Kawasaki	www.kawasaki.com/
Moto Guzzi	www.motoguzzi.it/
Suzuki	www.suzukicycles.com/
Triumph	www.triumph.co.uk/
Yamaha	www.yamaha-motor.com/

Auto Sites

There are many more auto sites run by enthusiasts, but the quality can vary enormously.

Autolink (UK) Limited – Links	www.autolinkuk.co.uk/clubs.htm
Cars Classics	www.cars.classics.co.uk/
Classic Car Directory	www.classicdirect.co.uk/
Classic Motor Monthly	www.classicmotor.co.uk/

Drive	www.drive.com.au/
iMotors.com	www.imotors.com/
Motor Trend	www.motortrend.com/
Motoring links	www.spartan-oc.demon.co.uk/links.htm
Net Car Links Page	www.netcar.co.uk/links.html
On Your Marques	www.288online.co.uk/classiccars
Team Net	www.team.net/
Yahoo	www.yahoo.com/recreation/automotive

Bike Sites

Bikers are a loyal bunch and this is reflected in their websites depicting their favourite bike.

All About Cycles	www.allaboutcycles.com/
AMA Superbike	www.amasuperbike.com/
Bike Net	www.bikenet.com/
BikeNet	www.bikenet.co.uk/
Bikedata	www.bikedata.co.uk/
BMW Bikes	www2.tower.org/bmwsite
British Motorcyclists Federation	www.bmf.co.uk/
Classic & Motorcycle Mechanics	dialspace.dial.pipex.com/mechanics/
Cycle Highway	www.cyclehighway.com/
Cycle News	www.cyclenews.com/
Longriders	www.longriders.com/

Motoplex	www.motoplex.com/
Motorbikes Online	www.motorbikes-online.com/
Motorcity.net	www.motorcity.net/
Motorcycle Action Group	mag-uk.org/
Motorcycle Online	www.motorcycle.com/
Motorcycle Travellers' Help	members.tripod.com/
Motorcycle USA	www.motorcycle-usa.com/
Motorcycle Web Index	sepnet.com/cycle
Motorcyclerow.com	www.motorcyclerow.com/
MotorcycleWorld	www.motorcycleworld.co.uk/
Motorsports Network	www.motorsports-network.com/
MotoWorld Network	www.motoworld.net/
Sidecar.com	www.sidecar.com/

In-Car Entertainment

I'm not sure whether it's a good idea to have all this gadgetery
under the driver's nose. In most countries it is an offence to have
a TV in the driver's view if the car is moving.

A Taste of Music	www.tasteofmusic.com/
Adler Audio	www.adleraudio.com/
Arocks Car Audio	www.arocks.com/
Audio Cyclone	www.audiocyclone.com/
Audio On Wheels	www.audioonwheels.com/
Auto Vibes	www.autovibes.com/
Bllamb Car Audio	www.bllamb.com/

Car Audio Index	**caraudioindex.com/**
Car Stereo Outlet	**www.carstereooutlet.com/**
Car Stereo World	**www.carstereoworld.com/**
Caraudio1	**www.caraudio1.com/**
Discount Auto Sound	**www.discountautosound.com/**
Discount Car Stereo Inc.	**www.discountcarstereo.com/**
Dynamic Auto Sounds	**www.dynamicautosounds.com/**
High Voltage Car Audio	**www.hvcamn.com/**

Just Car Audio	**www.justcaraudio.com/**
OnLine Car Stereo	**www.onlinecarstereo.com/**
Outlaw Audio	**www.outlawaudio.net/**
Radios and More	**www.radiosandmore.com/**
Sound Creations	**www.sound-creations.com/**

SoundDomain.com	www.sounddomain.com/
Stereo Direct	www.stereodirect.com/
Sweet Audio	www.sweetaudio.com/
The Car Stereo Connection	www.carstereoconnection.com/
Tune-Town	www.tune-town.com/
Ultimate Sounds	www.ultimate-sounds.com/

Insurance

Whether you're driving a car or a bike, third-party liability is a requirement. Phoning around insurance companies to get the best quote is an annual drudge, but the Internet can make it a little more pleasant. Some companies offer online quotations.

AA	www.aainsurance.co.uk/
Admiral	www.admiral.uk.com/
Bell Direct	www.belldirect.co.uk/
Car Quote	www.carquote.co.uk/
CGU	www.cgudirect.co.uk/
Diamond	www.diamond.uk.com/
Direct Line	www.directline.com/
Eagle Star Direct	www.eaglestardirect.co.uk/
Norwich Union Direct	www.norwichuniondirect.co.uk/
Quoteline Direct	www.nwnet.co.uk/wilsons
Royal Sun Alliance	www.royalsunalliance.com/
Screentrade	www.screentrade.com/

Leasing

The cost doesn't end when you've bought a car. There's servicing and repairs, and finally you've got the hassle of selling it when you need/like something different. Leasing a car overcomes all of this.

AMA www.vehiclecontracts.co.uk/

AVC Rent-A-Car www.all-vehicles.co.uk/

Brooklands www.brooklands-group.co.uk/

Car Myke www.carmyke.co.uk/

City Contracts www.citycontracts.co.uk/

DVC www.dvc-contracthire.co.uk/

Fairway www.fairway-leasing.com/

Fleetlease www.fleetlease.co.uk/

Fulton www.fultonnetwork.co.uk/

West Midlands Vehicles www.westmidvehicles.co.uk/

Motoring Organisations

In case of breakdown, it's advisable to belong to an organisation which will recover your car and get you to your destination.

AAA www.aaa.com/

Automobile Association www.theaa.co.uk/

BSM www.bsm.co.uk/
Green Flag www.greenflag.co.uk/
Institute of Advanced Motorists www.iam.org.uk/
RAC www.rac.co.uk/

News

To keep abreast of all the motoring news and views, there is a plethora of magazines and papers, many of which are now on the web.

Auto Channel www.theautochannel.com/
Auto Express www.autoexpress.co.uk/
Auto.com www.auto.com/
Autovantage www.autovantage.com/
Autoweb www.autoweb.com/
BBC Top Gear www.topgear.beeb.com/ homepage/
BMW Car Magazine www.bmwcarmagazine.com/
Car and Driver Magazine Online www.caranddriver.com/
Car Connection www.thecarconnection.com/
Car Magazine www.carmagazine.co.uk/
Cartalk www.cartalk.com/
Classic Car World www.classiccarworld.co.uk/
Classic Motor www.classicmotor.co.uk/
Final Lap www.finallap.com/
Microsoft Carpoint carpoint.msn.com/

Motor Cycle World Magazine	www.motorcycleworld.co.uk/
Motorsports Journal Online	www.motorsportsjournal.com/
Off-Road.com	www.off-road.com/
Victory Lane Magazine	www.victorylane.com/
Xtra Motoring Network	www.autonews.co.nz/

Owners' Clubs

Owners of classic cars frequently can't get spares from the usual sources and some spares are all but impossible to buy. This is where a club dedicated to a particular model can be invaluable.

Aston Martin Owners' Club	www.amoc.org/
BMC Car Parts	www.cars.classics.co.uk/adverts/car/bmc.html
Classic Car Owners' Clubs	www.288online.co.uk/classiccars/clubs.htm
DeLorean One	www.deloreanone.com/
Ford Classic and Capri Owners' Club	www.mistral.co.uk/pipes/fccoc.html
Holden Owners	www.holden4wdclubsa.asn.au/
Idaho Corvette Page	www.idavette.net/
Jensen Owners	www.british-steel.org/
North West Italian Car Owners' Club	www.provider.co.uk/users/hystericsoft/nw-italian-owners
Norton Owners' Club	www.noc.co.uk/
Old English Car Club	www.islandnet.com/~oecc/oecc.htm

Rolls Royce – Owners' Club	www.rroc.org/
Rolls Royce and Bentley	www.rrab.com/
Sunbeam Tiger Owner Association	www.engravers.com/tiger
The MG Cars Webring	www.mgcars.org.uk/webring
The UK Motor Sport Index	www.ukmotorsport.com/groups.html
Triumph Owners	www.harding.co.uk/triumph
UK Car Owners' Clubs	www.ukmotorsport.com/uk_car_clubs.html

Parts & Accessories

All cars need spares and third parties frequently produce parts which are as good as the manufacturer's original equipment, but a lot cheaper. There's also a big market in accessories.

Auto Vogue	www.autovogue.com/
Beltronics	www.beltronics.com/
Carbug	www.carbug.co.uk/
Euro Car Parts	www.eurocarparts.com/
Haynes Manuals	www.haynes.co.uk/
Kenwood	www.kenwood-electronics.co.uk/
Kwik-Fit	www.kwik-fit.com/
National Tyres	www.national.co.uk/
Navtrak	www.navtrak.com/
Superchips	www.superchips.co.uk/
Tire Rack	www.tirerack.com/

Trackstar	www.ractrackstar.co.uk/
VDO Dayton	www.vdodayton.com/
Vehix	www.vehix.com/

Petrol

To find out more about the stuff that propels your car or bike, visit one of these sites.

Amoco/BP	www.bpamoco.com/
Esso	www.esso.co.uk/
Shell	www.shell.com/
Texaco	www.texaco.com/
Total/Fina/Elf	www.totalfinaelf.com/

Registration Plates

It's a peculiarly British thing: getting a registration plate that reads something – the name of the driver or car. The costs can be very high.

| DVLA | www.dvla-som.co.uk/ |
| Ne-Numbers | www.ne-numbers.co.uk/ |

Registration Plates	www.regplate.com/
Registration Transfers	www.regtransfers.co.uk/
Speedy Registrations	www.speedyregistrations.co.uk/

Rental

For the odd occasion, a hired car is the answer.

Avis Rent A Car	www.avis.com/
BCR Car and Van Rental	www.bcvr.co.uk/
Classic Car Hire	www.classic-car-hire.co.uk/
Craven Classic Car Hire	www.yorkshirenet.co.uk/visinfo/ccch/
Easy Rentacar	www.easyrentacar.com/
Hertz Rent A Car	www.hertz.com/
Otis	www.otisvehiclerentals.co.uk/

Trading Autos

Buying and selling cars either privately or through dealers is the theme of this section.

Auto Trader	www.autotrader.co.uk/
Autobytel	www.autobytel.com/
Autoexchange	www.autoexchange.co.uk/
Autohit	www.autohit.com/
Autohunter	www.autohunter.co.uk/
Autopig	www.autopig.com/
Autotrader	www.autotrader.com/
Bristol Street Motors	www.bristolstreet.co.uk/
Buy a BMW	www.buyabmw.co.uk/
Buy a Mercedes	www.buyamercedes.co.uk/

Car Credit	www.yescarcredit.net/
Car Prices	www.carprices.com/
Car Sauce	www.carsauce.co.uk/
Carbusters	www.carbusters.com/
Carclub.com	www.carclub.com/
Cars.com	www.cars.com/
Carsdirect	www.carsdirect.com/
Carshop	www.carshop.co.uk/
Dixon Motors	www.dixonmotors.co.uk/
Economy Cars	www.ecomcars.co.uk/
Euro Car Consultants	www.eurocar.uk.com/
Fish 4 Cars	www.fish4cars.co.uk/
Go Brussels	www.gobrussels.com/
IntelliChoice Car Center	www.intellichoice.com/
KSB	www.ksb.co.uk/
Motor Nation	www.motornation.co.uk/
P&O	www.posl.com/
Parkers Guide	www.parkers.co.uk/
Planet Moto	www.planetmoto.co.uk/
Signature	www.signature.uk.com/
Trade Sales	www.trade-sales.co.uk/
What Car	www.whatcar.co.uk/
Wundercars	www.wundercars.co.uk/
Wykehams	www.wykehams.com/

Trading Bikes

Buying and selling bikes is just as popular as buying and selling cars. There's no shortage of websites around the world and it's a great deal more pleasurable than visiting each store in person.

Bike Trader	**www.biketrader.co.uk/**
Bike Mart	**www.bikemart.com/**
Cyber Cycles	**www.cybercycles.co.uk/**
Motor City	**www.motorcity.net/**

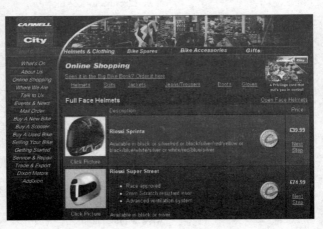

Motor Cycle City   **www.motorcycle-city.co.uk/**

Tyres

All you have is four bits of rubber (or two if you're on a bike) about the size of the sole of a man's shoe in contact with the ground. Better make sure they're good bits of rubber.

A1 Tyres	www.a1tyres.co.uk/
Alpha Tyres	www.alphatyres.com/
ATS Southern	www.ats-southern-motorcycle-tyres.co.uk/
Bridgestone Tyres	www.bridgestone-tyres.com/

Dunlop Tyres UK	www.dunloptyres.co.uk/
EDT	www.tyres-sold-online.co.uk/
Goodyear GB	www.goodyear.com/uk/
Just Tyres	www.justtyres.co.uk/
Kwik-Fit	www.kwik-fit.com/
Michelin	www.michelin.com/

National Tyre Distributors Assoc.	www.ntda.co.uk/
National Tyres	www.national.co.uk/
Pirelli Tyres	www.pirelli.com/
Redpath Tyres	www.redpath-tyres.co.uk/
Romac Tyres	www.romactyres.bizhosting.com/
Sinton Tyres	www.sintontyres.co.uk/
Tyre Trade News	www.tyretradenews.co.uk/
Tyres-Online	www.tyres-online.co.uk/

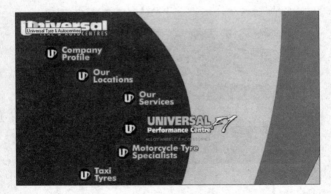

Universal Tyres	www.universal-tyres.co.uk/
Vintage Tyre Supplies	www.vintage-tyres.com/

Music

Whether you play an instrument or press the button of a CD player, there is plenty of scope on the Internet to stimulate your ears.

CD, Vinyl & Minidisc

The number of websites selling CDs seem to come second only to those selling books. There are some excellent deals to be had and the delivery is frequently very fast.

101CD	www.101cd.com/
13th Floor Company	www.13thfloorcompany.com/
Abbey Records	www.abbeyrecords.com/
ABC Music	www.abcmusic.co.uk/
Action Records	www.action-records.co.uk/
Amazon	www.amazon.com/
Audiostreet	www.audiostreet.com/
Beat Museum	www.thebeatmuseum.com/
Black Music	www.blackmail.com/
Blockbuster	www.blockbuster.co.uk/

Blues & Rhythm	www.bluesworld.com/BnR
BOL	www.bol.com/
Britannia Music and Video	www.britanniamusic.co.uk/
CD Now	www.cdnow.com/

CD-Wow	www.cd-wow.com/
Classical Choice	www.cdchoice.com/
Classical Insites	www.classicalinsites.com/
Compact Classics	www.compactclassics.co.uk/
Crotchet	www.crotchet.co.uk/
Dotmusic	www.dotmusic.com/
E-Dance	www.e-dance.co.uk/
Entertainment Express	www.entexpress.com/
Hard To Find Records	www.htfr.co.uk/
HMV	www.hmv.co.uk/
Internet Music Shop	www.musicsales.co.uk/
Jungle.com	www.jungle.com/
MDC Classic	www.mdcmusic.co.uk/
Ministry of Sound	www.ministryofsound.co.uk/
Moving Music	www.movingmusic.co.uk/
Music 365	www.music365.com/

Music Box	www.musicbox.uk.com/
Music Capital	www.musiccapital.com/
Music Metropolis	www.musicmetropolis.com/
Music Stop	www.music-stop.co.uk/
Musicmania	www.musicmania.co.uk/
New World Music	www.newworldmusic.com/
NME	www.nme.com/
Online Records	www.onlinerecords.co.uk/
Past Perfect	www.pastperfect.com/
Plantagenet Music	www.plantagenetmusic.co.uk/
Recollections	www.recollections.co.uk/
Record Store	www.recordstore.co.uk/
Seaford Music	www.seaford-music.co.uk/
Sentimental Records	www.sentimentalrecords.com/
Shop DVD	www.shopdvd.co.uk/
Sounds Great Music	www.soundsgreatmusic.com/
The Lobby	www.thelobby.co.uk/
The Muse	www.themuse.co.uk/
Timewarp Records	www.tunes.co.uk/timewarp
Tower Records UK	www.towerrecords.co.uk/
Uptown Records	www.uptownrecords.com/
VCI	www.vci.co.uk/
Vinyl Tap Records	www.vinyltap.co.uk/
Virgin Megastore	www.virginmega.com/

WH Smith Online – CD Channel   **cds.whsmithonline.co.uk/**

Ynot Music   **www.ynotmusic.co.uk/**

Musical Instruments

If it's a musical instrument you're after, or you want some help with playing, try visiting one of these sites.

2000 Gibson	**www.gibson.com/**
ABC Music	**www.abcmusic.co.uk/**
Aboriginal Art of Australia	**www.ozemail.com.au/~hallpa/**
Action Guitar	**www.actionguitar.com/**
Al Brisco's Steel Guitars	**www.steelguitarcanada.com/**
Alamo Music Center	**www.alamomusic.com/**
Bill's Music House	**www.billsmusic.com/**
Bluegrass in Scotland	**www.ednet.co.uk/~russell/**
BPM Music Express	**www.bpmmusic.com/**
Canada – Maestronet	**www.maestronet.com/**
Carter Steel Guitars	**www.steelguitar.com/**
Caruso Music Online	**www.caruso.net/**
Chamberlain Music	**www.chamberlainmusic.com/**
Churchill's Music	**www.churchills-music.co.uk/**
Conway Music Company	**www.conwaymusic.com/**

Dietze Music House	www.dietze.com/
Elderly Instruments	www.elderly.com/
FolkCraft Instruments	www.folkcraft.com/
Fred's Music Shop	www.fredsmusic.com/
Freehold Music Center	www.freeholdmusic.com/
General Music	www.generalmusic.com/
Giardinelli	www.giardinelli.com/
Guitar	www.guitar.com/
Guitar (Bob's)	www.guitarbob.com/
Guitar Chords	www.ws64.com/guitarchords/
Guitar World Online	www.guitarworld.com/
Harry Kolbe Soundsmith	www.soundsmith.com/
Hart Dynamics	www.hartdynamics.com/

| Hurdygurdy | www.hurdygurdy.com/ |
| International Saxophone | www.saxophone.org/ |

K&K Music	www.kandkmusic.com/
King Music Inc.	www.kingmusic.com/
Lone Star Percussion	www.lonestarpercussion.com/
Long & McQuade	www.long-mcquade.com/
Mandala – Beyond A Lucid State	www.progressive-music.com/
Marsha Taylor Oboe Products	www.oboe.org/
McCabe's Guitar Shop	www.mccabesguitar.com/
MIDI Wind Controllers FAQ	www.harmony-central.com/midi/doc/wind-controllers.txt
Midi.com	www.midi.com/

Midwest Musical Imports	www.mmimports.com/
Music and Audio Connection	www.musicandaudio.com/
Music Connection	www.the-music-connection.com/
Music Industries	www.musicindustries.com/
Music Resources – Sibelius Academy	www.siba.fi/Kulttuuripalvelut/music.html
National Educational Music Company	www.nemc.com/
Optek Music Systems, Inc.	www.optekmusic.com/
Organ Supply Industries	www.organsupply.com/
Paul Reed Smith Guitars	www.prsguitars.com/
Pensa Custom Guitars	www.pensaguitars.com/
Percussive Arts Society	www.pas.org/
Powell Flutes	www.powellflutes.com/
Rocky Mountain Music	www.rockymountainmusic.com/
Roland US	www.rolandus.com/
Rose-Morris Music Store	www.rose-morris.co.uk/
Santa Cruz Guitar Company	www.santacruzguitar.com/
Selmer Musical Instruments	www.selmer.com/
Smith-Watkins Brass	www.rsmi.u-net.com/
Sound Beat UK	www.soundbeat.mcmail.com/
Studio Instrument Rentals	www.sirny.com/
The Piano Page	www.ptg.org/
The Recorder	www.iinet.net.au/~nickl/recorder.html
Trumpet Player Online	www.v-zone.com/tpo

Tutti	www.tutti.co.uk/
Uilleann.com	www.uilleann.com/
Used Guitar	www.usedguitar.com/
Vintage Drum Center	www.vintagedrum.com/
Viola da Gamba Society	www.vdgs.demon.co.uk/
Washington Music Center	www.wmcworld.com/
West Music	www.westmusic.com/
Wichita Band Instrument Co.	www.wichitaband.com/
Wink Music World Sounds	www.winkworldsounds.com/

MP3

MP3 is a file format for compressed digital music files. You need an MP3 player for your PC and then you can download digital music from the Internet and play it on your computer. If you want to play it on something rather more portable than your computer, you can buy a battery powered portable MP3 player.

MP3 Players

| MP3 Players & Tools | www.mysharewarepage.com/ mp3.htm |

| Sonique | www.sonique.com/ |
| Xing | www.xingtech.com/ |

MP3 Music Files

Abstract MP3	www.abstractmp3s.com/
Access Music Network	www.a-m-n.com/index.asp
Audio Find	www.audiofind.com/
BURBs	www.burbs.co.uk/
Crunch	www.crunch.co.uk/
Fast MP3 Search	mp3.lycos.com/
Hot MP3s	members.xoom.com/mp3_suite/
Hungry Bands	www.hungrybands.com/
Metacrawler	www.palavista.com/
MP3 Bot Search Engine	www.informatch.com/mediabot/
MP3 Central	music.lycos.com/mp3
MP3 MTV Hits	come.to/mp3mtvhits
MP3 Now	www.mp3now.com/

MP3.com	www.MP3.com/
MP4 music	www.mp4music.com/
Music Match	www.musicmatch.com/
Palavista Digital Music	www.palavista.com/
RioPort	www.rioport.com/
Technomusic	www.technomusic.com/
Tony's International MP3	www.funaki.com/Tony/mp3/
Vitaminic	www.vitaminic.com/

Orchestras

Adelaide Symphony Orchestra	www.aso.com.au/
Association of British Orchestras	www.orchestranet.co.uk/abo.html
BBC Philharmonic Orchestra	www.bbc.co.uk/orchestras/philharmonic/
BBC Symphony Orchestra	www.bbc.co.uk/orchestras
Bristol Concert Orchestra	www.bristolconcertorchestra.org.uk/
Cyber Symphony Orchestra	www.cyber-symphony.com/
Edinburgh Symphony Orchestra	uk.geocities.com/edinburghso
Glasgow Chamber Orchestra	gco.freeservers.com/
Irish Chamber Orchestra	www.icorch.com/
Kensington Symphony Orchestra	ds.dial.pipex.com/town/close/yl32/
London Metropolitan Orchestra	www.lmo.co.uk/
London Philharmonic Orchestra	www.lpo.co.uk/
London Symphony Orchestra	www.lso.co.uk/
Metropolitan Symphony Orch.	www.msoa.net/
National Association of Youth Orchestras	www.nayo.org.uk/
National Youth Orchestra of Great Britain	www.btinternet.com/~nyo/
New Edinburgh Orchestra	www.ndirect.co.uk/~williams/neo/
New Zealand Symphony Orch.	www.nzso.co.nz/
Philadelphia Orchestra	www.philorch.org/

Philharmonia Orchestra	www.philharmonia.co.uk/
Royal Liverpool Philharmonic Orchestra	rlps.merseyworld.com/
Royal Philharmonic Orchestra	www.orchestranet.co.uk/rpo.html
Royal Scottish National Orchestra	www.scot-art.org/rsno/
Seattle Symphony Orchestra	www.seattlesymphony.org/
Studio Symphony Orchestra	www.users.globalnet.co.uk/~asg/

Stars' Websites

Fanclubs can be very lucrative for the stars, but most are there just to keep fans up-to-date with the singer or the group, forthcoming concerts and record releases.

ABBA	www.abbasite.com/
Barry Manilow	www.manilow.com/
Beach Boys	surf.to/the.beach.boys
Beatles	www.beatles.com/
Billy Joel	www.sonymusic.com/artists/BillyJoel/
Blondie	www.blondie.net/
Bonnie Tyler	www.bonnietyler.com/main.html
Bread	www.ktb.net/~insync/breadtitle.html
Britney Spears	www.britneyspears.org/
Bryan Adams	www.bryanadams.com/
Carly Simon	www.carlysimon.com/
Cat Stevens	catstevens.com/

Cilla Black	www.cillablack.com/
Cyndi Lauper	www.cyndilauper.com/
David Bowie	www.davidbowie.com/
Don McLean	www.don-mclean.com
Elton John	www.eltonjohn.com/
Elvis Presley	www.elvis-presley.com/
Geri Halliwell	www.geri-halliwell.com/
Janet Jackson	www.janet-online.com/
Joan Baez	www.baez.woz.org/
Johnny Cash	www.johnnycash.com/
Kenny Ball & His Jazzmen	www.kennyball.com/
Lisa Stansfield	www.lisa-stansfield.com/
Madonna	www.madonnafanclub.com/
Marc Bolan	www.marc-bolan.net/
Mariah Carey	www.mariahcarey-fanclub.com/
Martine McCutcheon	www.martinemccutcheon.com/
Michael Bolton	www.michaelbolton-fanclub.com/
Michael Jackson	www.mjnet.com/
Mike Oldfield	www.mikeoldfield.org/
Neil Diamond	www.neildiamondhomepage.com/
Paul Simon	www.wbr.com/paulsimon/
Pete Townsend	www.petetownshend.co.uk/
Procol Harum	www.procolharum.com/
Rolling Stones	www.stones.com/

Roy Orbison	www.orbison.com/
Roy Wood	www.roywood.co.uk/
Queen	queen-fip.com/
Simply Red	www.simplyred.co.uk/
Status Quo	www.statusquo.co.uk/
Suzi Quatro	www.ozemail.com.au/~suziq/
Tina Turner	www.tina-turner.com/

Unofficial Sites

In addition to the 'official' websites of the stars, there are also many unofficial ones which have been put together by loyal fans.

ABBA	www.abbasite.com/
Artist Information	www.artistinformation.com/
Badfinger	hjem.get2net.dk/Badfinger
Black Sabbath	www.inx.de/~arack/bsfcd.html
Britney Spears	www.artistinformation.com/ britney_spears.html
Diana Ross	www.dianaross.com/
Dusty Springfield	www.dustyspringfield.nu/
Electric Light Orchestra	clix.to/elo
Elvis Presley	www.elvis.com/
Eric Clapton Fanzine	www.xs4all.nl/~slowhand
Everly Brothers	www.everly.net/
Frankie Valli	www.srv.net/~roxtar/ valli_frankie.html

Kinks	hobbes.it.rit.edu/kinks/kinks.html
Kylie Minogue	www.kylie.com/
Linda Wong	members.aol.com/bearpage/linda/

Monkees	www.themonkees.com/
Olivia Newton-John	www.onlyolivia.com/
Online Talent	www.onlinetalent.com/
Phil Collins	home.snafu.de/dito/takehome.htm
Shadows	home.online.no/~jaflatby/
Spice Girls	c3.vmg.co.uk/spicegirls/

News

The Internet can provide all the news you want to keep abreast of the latest worldwide developments.

Magazines

There are countless magazines and periodicals published throughout the world and many of them are also available on the Internet.

Astronomy Now	www.astronomynow.com/
Bike Net Magazine	www.bikenet-magazine.com/
Bizarre Magazine	www.bizarremag.com/
BMJ Medical Journal	www.bmj.com/
British Magazines Direct	www.britishmagazines.com/
CADCAM Magazine	www.cadcam-magazine.co.uk/
Car and Driver	www.caranddriver.com/
Career Magazine	www.careermag.com/
Cosmopolitan	www.cosmomag.com/
Data Communications Magazine	www.data.com/
Economist, The	www.economist.com/

Fast Car	www.fastcar.co.uk/
Feed Magazine	www.feedmag.com/
Glamour Magazine	www.glamourmagazine.co.uk/
GQ	www.gq-magazine.co.uk/
Halloween Magazine	www.halloween-magazine.com/
Hello!	www.hello-magazine.co.uk/
InteracTive	www.questpub.co.uk/
Little Magazines	www.little-magazines.org.uk/
Lobster	www.lobster-magazine.co.uk/
Maxim	www.maxim-magazine.co.uk/
Men's Health	www.menshealth.com/
Motor Cycle Online	www.motorcycle.com/
Motor Trend Online	www.motortrend.com/
National Enquirer Online	www.nationalenquirer.com/
National Geographic	www.nationalgeographic.com/
Nature	www.nature.com/
New Scientist Planet Science	www.newscientist.com/
Plants Magazine	www.plants-magazine.com/
Prospect Magazine	www.prospect-magazine.co.uk/
Q Magazine	www.q4music.com/
Riviera Magazine	www.riviera-magazine.com/
Rolling Stone Magazine	www.rollingstone.com/
Royalty	www.royalty-magazine.com/
Salon	www.salon.com/
Science Daily Magazine	www.sciencedaily.com/

Scientific American	**www.sciam.com**/
Sky Magazine	**www.skymagazine.co.uk**/
Smash Hits	**www.smashhits.net**/

TIME.com	**www.time.com**/
Time Out	**www.timeout.com**/
Time Out – Brussels	**www.timeout.com/brussels**/
Time Out – Budapest	**www.timeout.com/budapest**/
Time Out – Chicago	**www.timeout.com/chicago**/
Time Out – Dublin	**www.timeout.com/dublin**/
Time Out – London	**www.timeout.com/london**/
Time Out – New York	**www.timeoutny.com**/

Time Out – Paris	www.timeout.com/paris/
Time Out – Prague	www.timeout.com/prague/
Time Out – Rome	www.timeout.com/rome/
Uploaded	www.uploaded.com/
Wallpaper	www.wallpaper.com/

Newspapers

Instead of reading the news on paper, you can log onto the newspaper's website. It's all very clever, but I still think paper is easier to read than a screen.

ABC Rural Bush Telegraph (AU)	www.abc.net.au/rural/
Australia Daily (AU)	www.ausdaily.net.au/
Australian Financial Review (AU)	www.afr.com.au/
Belfast Telegraph (UK)	www.belfasttelegraph.co.uk/
Big Issue, The (UK)	www.bigissue.com/
Canberra Times (AU)	www.canberratimes.com.au/
Chicago Tribune (US)	www.chicagotribune.com/
Christchurch Press Online (NZ)	www.press.co.nz/
Coventry Evening Telegraph (UK)	www.go2coventry.co.uk/
Daily Express (UK)	express.lineone.net/
Daily Record and Sunday Mail (UK)	www.record-mail.co.uk/rm/
Dallas Morning News (US)	www.dallasnews.com/
Electronic Telegraph (UK)	www.telegraph.co.uk/
Evening Chronicle (UK)	www.evening-chronicle.co.uk/

Evening Gazette (UK)	www.eveninggazette.co.uk/
Evening Telegraph (UK)	www.dcthomson.co.uk/mags/tele
Financial Times (UK)	www.ft.com/
Guardian, The (UK)	www.guardian.co.uk/
Independent, The (UK)	www.independent.co.uk/
Ireland on Sunday (IE)	www.irelandonsunday.com/
Ireland Today (IE)	www.ireland-today.ie/
Irish Echo (IE)	www.irishecho.com/index.cfm
Irish Independent (IE)	www.independent.ie/
Irish News (IE)	www.irishnews.com/
Irish News (UK)	www.irishnews.com/
Irish Post (UK)	www.irishpost.co.uk/
Irish Regional Newspapers Online (IE)	www.rmbi.ie/
Irish Times (IE)	www.ireland.com/
Irish Voice Online (IE)	www.irishvoice.com/
Irish World (IE)	www.theirishworld.com/
Limerick Leader Online (IE)	www.limerick-leader.ie/
London Daily (UK)	www.london-daily.com/
London Evening Standard (UK)	www.thisislondon.com/
Los Angeles Times (US)	www.latimes.com/
Mirror Online (UK)	www.mirror.co.uk/
Montreal Gazette (CA)	www.montrealgazette.com/
New York Daily News (US)	www.nydailynews.com/
New York Post (US)	www.nypostonline.com/

New York Times (US)	www.nytimes.com/
Otago Daily Times (NZ)	www.odt.co.nz/
Philadelphia Inquirer (US)	www.phillynews.com/inq
Pittsburgh Tribune-Review (US)	triblive.com/
Private Eye (UK)	www.private-eye.co.uk/
San Francisco Chronicle (US)	www.sfgate.com/chronicle
San Francisco Examiner (US)	www.examiner.com/
Scotsman, The (UK)	www.scotsman.com/
Seattle Times (US)	www.seattletimes.com/
Sporting Life (UK)	www.sportinglife.co.uk/
Sun, The (UK)	www.the-sun.co.uk/
Sunday Mirror (UK)	www.sundaymirror.co.uk/
Sunday People (UK)	www.people.co.uk/
Sunday Post (UK)	www.sundaypost.com/
Sunday Sun (UK)	www.sundaysun.co.uk/
Sunday Times (UK)	www.sunday-times.co.uk/
Sydney Morning Herald (AU)	www.smh.com.au/
Telegraph Online (UK)	dspace.dial.pipex.com/town/square/de95
Times, The (UK)	www.the-times.co.uk/
Toronto Star (CA)	www.thestar.com/
Ulster Herald (UK)	www.ulsterherald.com/
USA Today (US)	www.usatoday.com/
Vancouver Sun (CA)	www.vancouversun.com/
Wall Street Journal (US)	www.wsj.com/

Washington Post (US)	**www.washingtonpost.com/**
Washington Times (US)	**www.washtimes.com/**
West Australian News Review (AU)	**www.perth-wa.com/**
Western Australian Business News (AU)	**www.businessnews.com.au/**
XTRA Today News (NZ)	**www.xtra.co.nz/news/index.html**

News

There are several other sources of news, including TV websites.

CNN Interactive	**www.cnn.com/**
Electronic Newsstand	**www.enews.com/**
ESPNet SportsZone	**espnet.sportszone.com/**
Excite Live!	**live.excite.com/**
Journalism UK	**www.octopod.demon.co.uk/ journ_uk.htm**
London News Network Online	**www.lnn-tv.co.uk/**
Lycos News	**news.lycos.de/news/uk/**
Mercury Center (San Jose Mercury News)	**www.sjmercury.com/**
MSN News	**www.msnbc.com/news**
News Bytes	**www.nbnn.com/**
NewsPage	**www.newpage.com/**
NPR on the Web	**npr.org/**
PoliticsNow	**www.politicsnow.com/**
PopSci.com	**www.popsci.com/**

Press Association	www.pa.press.net/
Reuters	www.reuters.com/
Suck	www.suck.com/

| USA Today | www.usatoday.com/ |

Weather

For some people the weather is a matter of extreme importance. Up-to-the-minute weather details are available round-the-clock, worldwide, from numerous Internet websites.

Airport Information & Weather	www.avnet.co.uk/tmdg/weather
Ant Veal's UK Weather Centre	web.bham.ac.uk/ggy4atv3/weather.htm
BBC Weather Centre	www.bbc.co.uk/weather

CNN.com — www.cnn.co.uk/

Intellicast – Europe Local Weather — www.intellicast.com/

Medium-Range Weather Forecasts — www.ecmwf.int/

Meteorology Office — www.meto.gov.uk/

Online Weather (UK) — www.onlineweather.com/

PA News Centre – Weather — www.paweathercentre.com/

Snow Sport World — www.snowsportworld.com/

The Weather Channel — www.weather.com/

Today's Weather Forecast — www.msn.co.uk/page/2-12.asp

UK Aviation Weather — www.pilotweb.co.uk/

UK Weather — www.pa.press.net/weather

UK Weather — www.uk-weather.co.uk/

Weather — uk.multimap.com/map/weather.cgi

Weather — www.guardianunlimited.co.uk/weather

Weather Glossary	www.geocities.com/heartland/1102/wxdefs.html
Weather Reports From Around the UK	www.meto.gov.uk/datafiles/the wx_uk.html
Weather.com	www.weather.com/intl/
Yahoo! Weather	uk.weather.yahoo.com/

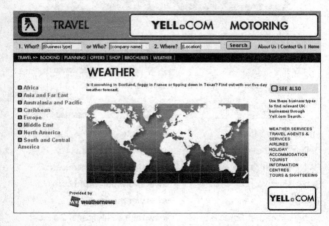

| Yellow Pages Weather | uk.yell.com/travel/weathe/ |

Pets

It has been proven that owning a pet, in particular a cat or a dog, is very beneficial. Dog and cat owners seem to live longer and are less stressed.

Pet Care

These sites deal in general pet supplies and pet issues. There are also a few which specialise in particular types of animals.

AKC	**www.akc.org/**
Animail	**www.animail.co.uk/**
Animal Network	**www.animalnetwork.com/**
Animal People	**www.animalpeople.com/**
Complete Hamster Guide	**www.hamsters.co.uk/**
Hartz	**www.hartz.com/**
Healthy Pet	**www.healthypet.com/**
High Hopes for Pets	**www.highhopes4pets.com/**
I Love My Pet	**www.ilovemypet.com/**
Iams	**www.iams.com/**
In Memory of Pets	**www.in-memory-of-pets.com/**

Kingsnake	www.kingsnake.com/
Net Pets	www.jetpets.com/
Netpets	www.netpets.com/
Noah's Pets	www.noahspets.com/
Ohare	www.ohare.org/
Paws	www.paws.org/
Pet Club	www.petclub.org/
Pet Co.	www.petco.com/
Pet Dental	www.petdental.com/
Pet Diabetes	www.petdiabetes.org/
Pet Emporium	www.petemporium.co.uk/
Pet Loss	www.petloss.com/
Pet Loves	www.petloves.com/
Pet Net	www.pet-net.net/
Pet of the Day	www.petoftheday.com/
Pet Planet	www.petplanet.co.uk/
Pet Shelter	www.petshelter.org/
Pet Station	www.petstation.com/
Pet Unlimited	www.petsunlimited.com/
Pet Vacations	www.petvacations.com/
Pet's Pyjamas	www.petspyjamas.com/
Petfinder	www.petfinder.org/
Petmarket	www.petmarket.com/
Petopia	www.petopia.com/

Petplan   **www.petplan.co.uk/**

Pets and People   **www.petsandpeople.com/**

Pets In Need

The First Private No-Kill Shelter Serving the Peninsula & Silicon Valley

873 Fifth Ave., Redwood City, CA 94063
(650) 367-1405

Pets In Need's mission is to bring a loving, healthy home within paw's reach of every adoptable dog and cat in our community. At the Pets In Need Shelter, no dog or cat suitable for re-homing is ever put to death, no matter how long it takes.

Pets in Need   **www.petsinneed.org/**

Pets Part of the Family   **www.petspartofthefamily.com/**

Pets Welcome   **www.petswelcome.com/**

Pets.com   **www.pets.com/**

Petsmart   **www.petsmart.com/**

Petz   **www.petz.co.uk/**

Power Paws   **www.powerpaws.com/**

SFB   **www.sfb.com/**

That Pet Place   **www.thatpetplace.com/**

The Pet Channel   **www.thepetchannel.com/**

Travel Pets   **www.travelpets.com/**

These sites deal specifically in one particular type of animal:

Birds

Birds 'N' Ways	www.birdsnways.com/
Birdtable	www.birdtable.com/
Fanciers	www.fanciers.com/
FC Aviary	www.fcaviary.com/
Parrot Parrot	www.parrotparrot.com/
Parrot Sanctuary	www.parrot-sanctuary.org/
Parrots and Company	www.parrotsandcompany.com/
Pet Parrot	www.petparrot.com/
Quaker Parrots	www.quakerparrots.com/

Cats

Cat Care Society	www.catcaresociety.org/

Cat Claws	www.catclaws.com/

Cat Company, The	www.thecatcompany.com/
Cat Faeries	www.catfaeries.com/
Cat Treasures	www.cattreasures.com/
Cats and Kittens	www.catsandkittens.com/
Cats and Rabbits and more	www.catsandrabbitsandmore.com/
Cats Magazine	www.catsmag.com/
Cute Cats	www.cutecats.com/
Dreamcats	www.dreamcats.com/
Feral Cat	www.feralcat.com/
I Love Cats	www.i-love-cats.com/

Dogs

Aaarf	www.aaarf.org/
Canismajor	www.canismajor.com/
Digital Dog	www.digitaldog.com/
Dog Breed Info	www.dogbreedinfo.com/
Dog.com	www.dog.com/
Dog Info	www.doginfo.com/
Dog-On-It	www.dog-on-it.com/
Dog Play	www.dog-play.com/
Dog Pro	www.dogpro.com/
Dog World Magazine	www.dogworldmag.com/
Dog Zone	www.dogzone.com/
Dogs Top	www.dogstop.com/
i-Dog	www.i-dog.com/

Infodog	www.infodog.com/
Pugs	www.pugs.com/
Sled Dog	www.sleddogcentral.com/
Travel Dog	www.traveldog.com/
Woofs – magazine	www.woofs.org/

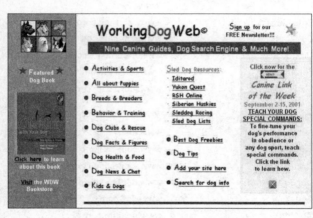

| Working Dog | www.workingdogweb.com/ |
| World Class Dogs | www.worldclassdogs.com/ |

Fish

Evolve Fish	www.evolvefish.com/
Fishlink Central	www.fishlinkcentral.com/
FishTalk	www.fishtalk.com/
Pet Fish	www.petfish.com/

Hamsters

British Hamster Society	web.ukonline.co.uk/g.forrest/hamster/society.htm
Caring for your Hamster	www.bsava.ac.uk/petzone/petcare/hamsters.htm
Complete Hamster Site	www.hamsters.co.uk/
Dylan Hamster Site	www.dylan.org/
Hamster Care	www.dhassa.co.uk/hamsters
Hamster Poster Page	www.users.globalnet.co.uk/~tvhams/poster1.html
Hamsters	www.the-hamsters.cx/
Heart of England Hamster Club	www.hamsters.co.uk/hoehc.htm
Minx Hamstery	www.minxlinx.co.uk/
South Of England Hamster Club	www.angelfire.com/ok/soehc/
Towy Vale Hamstery	www.towyvale.hamsters.btinternet.co.uk/

Rabbits

Bunny Luv	www.bunnyluv.com/
Cats and Rabbits and more	www.catsandrabbitsandmore.com/
House Rabbit	www.houserabbit.org/
Rabbit	www.rabbit.org/
Rabbit	www.rabbits.com/
Rabbit Web	www.rabbitweb.net/
Show Bunny	www.showbunny.com/

Reptiles

Caring for Reptiles or Amphibians	**pets.msn.com/morepets/reptiles/article7.asp**

Chameleons	**www.skypoint.com/members/mikefry/chams.html**
Pet Reptiles & Amphibians	**pets.msn.com/morepets/reptiles/default.asp**
Pets and Things	**www.petsandthings.com/**
Plated Lizards	**www.sonic.net/~melissk/plated.html**
Reptile Chatroom	**www.petsunlimited.com/pchat/reptile/**
Reptile Pet Specifics	**www.cvm.uiuc.edu/ceps/petcolumns/reptile_pets.html**
Reptiles and Amphibians	**www.vin.com/petcare/reptiles.htm**
Reptile Supplies	**www.worldwidepetsupply.com/worldwidepet/repsup.html**

Recruitment

Searching for a job can be a soul-destroying activity. The Internet can speed things up by allowing you to search for specific types of jobs.

Job Hunting

1 Jobs	www.1-jobs.com/
Antal International	www.antal-int.com/
APN Development Training	www.apn.co.uk/
Aupairs	www.aupairs.co.uk/
Big Blue Dog	www.bigbluedog.com/
Brainbench.com	www.brainbench.com/
Brassring	www.brassring.com/
BUNAC	www.bunac.org.uk/
Byron	www.byron.com.au/
Career Builder	www.careerbuilder.com/
Career Connections	www.career.com/
Career Exchange	www.careerexchange.com/
Career Magazine Online	www.careermag.com/

Career Mosaic	www.careermosaic.com/
Career Path	www.careerpath.com/
Careerlab.com	www.careerlab.com/
College Graduate Job Hunter	www.collegegrad.com/
Computer Jobs.com	www.computerjobs.com/
Cool Works	www.coolworks.com/
DICE	www.dice.com/
E-mum	www.e-mum.com/
Free agent.com	www.freeagent.com/
Freetimejobs.com	www.freetimejobs.com/
Guru.com	www.guru.com/
Head Hunter	www.headhunter.net/

Hot Jobs	www.hotjobs.com/
Job Options	www.joboptions.com/
Job.com	www.job.com/
Jobs at HP	www.jobs.hp.com/
Jobs Online	www.jobsonline.com/

Jobs UK	www.topjobs.net/
Jobs.com	www.jobs.com/
Jobsdb.com	www.jobsdb.com/
Jobsearch	www.jobsearch.gov.au/
JobServe	www.jobserve.com/
JobTrak	www.jobtrak.com/
JobWeb	www.jobweb.com/
London Careers	www.londoncareers.net/
Manpower	www.manpower.co.uk/
Monster.com	www.monster.com/
My Career	www.mycareer.com.au/
Nation Job Online	www.nationjob.com/
Net-temps	www.net-temps.com/
New Scientist Jobs.com	www.newscientistjobs.com/
Overseas Jobs Web	www.overseasjobs.com/
People Bank	www.peoplebank.co.uk/
Planet Recruit.com	www.planetrecruit.com/
Recruitability	www.recruitability.com/
Reed	www.reed.co.uk/
Retail Careers	www.retailcareers.co.uk/
Seek	www.seek.com.au/
Six Figure Income	www.sixfigureincome.com/
Summer Jobs	www.summerjobs.com/
Talent 2000	www.bbc.co.uk/education/lzone/talent2000/index.shtml

Techies.com	www.techies.com/
Top Jobs	www.topjobs.net/
Total Jobs	www.totaljobs.com/
UK Recruiters	www.nmib.com/
Vault.com	www.vault.com/
Wet Feet	www.wetfeet.com/

CV Writing

The first impression a prospective employer gets is usually from your Curriculum Vitae or Résumé. It's worth spending time on it.

CV Services Special	www.cvspecial.co.uk/
Free CV / résumé tips & advice	www.alec.co.uk/
Head-Hunters	www.users.dircon.co.uk/~cvextra/
Impression CVs	www.impressioncv.co.uk/
IT Jobs Online	www.it-jobs-online.co.uk/
Job Hunting Tips	www.haybrook.co.uk/tips.html
London University Careers Service	www.careers.lon.ac.uk/
Newmonday.com	r.lksm.com/
Professional CV Writing Service	www.bradleycvs.demon.co.uk/
Prospects	www.prospects.co.uk/
S-Multimedia	www.angelfire.com/biz2/smultimedia/index.html
Total CV Tips	www.totaljobs.com/

Reference

The Internet is a tremendous source of information about anything and everything. Because of the powerful search features, information can be located very quickly.

Encyclopedia

I can't imagine there's much that the average person would want to know that isn't here.

Bartleby.com	**www.bartleby.com/**
Comptons Home Library	**www.comptons.com/**
Conflict World Encyclopedia	**www.emulateme.com/**
Encarta Online	**encarta.msn.com/**
Encyberpedia	**www.encyberpedia.com/**
Encyclopedia	**www.encyclopedia.com/**
Encyclopedia Britannica	**www.britannica.com/**
Encyclopedia Britannica Online	**www.eb.com**
Encyclopedia Smithsonian	**www.si.edu/resource/faq/start.htm**
EncycloZine	**encyclozine.com/**

Expert Central	www.expertcentral.com/
Free Internet Encyclopedia	www.clever.net/cam/encyclopedia.html
Free Online Encyclopedia	www.theinfosphere.com/
Grup Encyclopedia Catalana	www.grec.net/home/grec/english/index.htm
Nolos Legal Encyclopedia	www.nolo.com/briefs.html
Nupedia	www.nupedia.com/
Virtual Encyclopedia	www.abp1.com/1getsmrt/index.html
World Book	www.worldbookonline.com/

General Knowledge

More information can be gleaned from these dictionaries, atlases and other sites of knowledge.

A Man's Life	www.manslife.com/
Acronyms	www.acronymfinder.com/
American Medical Association	www.ama-assn.org/
Big Book	www.bigbook.com/
Biography Online	www.biography.com/
City.Net	www.city.net/
City Search	www.citysearch.com/
Dictionary	www.dictionary.com/
Ditto	www.ditto.com/
eHow	www.ehow.com/
Electric Library	www.elibrary.com/

Flags	www.fotw.net/flags
Four11	www.four11.com/
Funk and Wagnall	www.funkandwagnalls.com/
Getty Thesaurus	shiva.pub.getty.edu/tgn_browser
Grammar	www.edunet.com/english/ grammar
Grove Dictionary of Art	www.groveart.com/
How Stuff Works	www.howstuffworks.com/
Internet FAQs	www.faqs.org/
Learn 2	www.learn2.com/
Look Smart	www.looksmart.com/
Map Quest	www.mapquest.com/
Merrium-Webster	www.m-w.com/
Mythology	www.pantheon.org/mythica
NASA	www.nasa.gov/
National Geographic	www.nationalgeographic.com/
One Look Dictionary	www.onelook.com/
Scholastic Network	www.scholastic.com/
Scientific American	www.sciam.com/

The Why Files	whyfiles.news.wisc.edu/
World CIA Factbook	www.odci.gov/cia/publications/ factbook
World of Flags	www.flagwire.com/

Libraries

If you want a book for reference, use a library.

British Library	**www.bl.uk/**
Library of Congress	**www.loc.gov/**
New York Public library	**www.nypl.org/**

Finding Out

There is a great deal of information that can be tracked down on the Internet, from train times to the whereabouts of your local plumber.

Allexperts.com	**www.allexperts.com/**
Info Please	**www.infoplease.com/**
Post Office Counters Ltd	**www.postoffice-counters.co.uk/**
Railtrack: Travel Information	**www.railtrack.co.uk/**
Scoot	**www.scoot.co.uk/**
TheTrainline.com	**www.thetrainline.com/**
The Weather Channel	**www.weather.com/**
The Yellow Pages (UK)	**www.yell.co.uk/**
The Yellow Pages (US)	**www.yell.com/**
Timetables	**www.rail.co.uk/ukrail/planner/ planner.htm**
UK Directory Enquiries	**www.192.com/**
UK Public Transport Information	**www.pti.org.uk/**

Maps

If you want to find out where you are, or where you'd like to be, use the Internet to look it up. Just about every square inch of the planet is covered.

Absolute Authority on Cartography	www.absoluteauthority.com/cartography
Amazing Picture Machine	www.ncrtec.org/picture.htm
Articque	www.articque.com/
Atlantic Ocean	geography.miningco.com/library/maps/blatlantic.htm
Atlapedia Online	www.atlapedia.com/
Atlas of the World	cliffie.nosc.mil/~natlas/
Carta-Graphics	www.carta-graphics.com/
Cartesia MapResources	www.map-art.com/
Cartographic Resources	130.166.124.2/cart.html
Clover Point Cartographics	www.cloverpoint.com/
Creative Force Inc	www.creativeforceinc.com/
Cyber Atlas	www.cyberatlas.com/
DeLorme	www.delorme.com/
Digital Cartographics	www.digitalcarto.com/
Digital Cartography	www.digiatlas.com/ang
Digital City	home.digitalcity.com/maps/
Digital Data Services	ddsllc.com/gis.htm
Digital Wisdom	www.digital-wisdom.org/

Dreamline Cartography	pw2.netcom.com/~animated/main.html
Earth Resources Observation	edcwww.cr.usgs.gov/
Electronic Map Library	130.166.124.2/library.html
ESRI	www.esri.com/
Eureka Cartography	www.maps-eureka.com/
Frog Heaven Maps	www.frogheaven.com/
GeoCommunity	www.geocomm.com/
GeoMapping	www.geomapping.com/
GeoPlace	www.geoplace.net/
Geoplaning	www.geoplaning.com/
Graphic Maps	www.graphicmaps.com/aatlas/world.htm
Great Globe Gallery	main.amu.edu.pl/~zbzw/glob/glob1.htm
Imagemaps from Wildgoose	www.imagemapuk.com/
International Map Trade Association	maptrade.org/
KennKart Digital Mapping	www3.sympatico.ca/kennkart
Kingfisher Maps and Charts	www.kfmaps.com/
Location Maps	www.finders-uk.co.uk/
Map Machine	www.nationalgeographic.com/maps/
Map World	www.mapworld.com/
Mapcraft Custom Cartography	www.mapcraft.com/
MapHist Discussion Group	www.maphist.nl/

MapMart	www.mapmart.com/
MapQuest!	www.mapquest.com/
Maps of the Solar System	maps.jpl.nasa.gov/
Maps of the States	welcome.to/states_maps
Maps.com	www.maps.com/
Mercator's World	www.mercatormag.com/
National Geographic Society	www.nationalgeographic.com/
National Imagery and Mapping Agency	www.nima.mil/
Quick Maps	www.theodora.com/maps/ abc_world_maps.html
Rustbelt Cartography	www.rustbelt.com/
Scale Finder	www.onthelimit.freeuk.com/
Solid Terrain Modeling	www.solidterrainmodeling.com/
Spellex Geographical Dictionary Software	www.spellex.com/geo1.htm
Streetmap UK	www.streetmap.co.uk/
Streetmap USA	www.streetmap.com/
Tercomp	www.tercomp.it/
TerraServer	www.terraserver.com/
U.S. Geological Survey	www.usgs.gov/
USGS National Mapping Info.	mapping.usgs.gov/
Versamap Digital Mapping	www.versamap.com/
Washington Map Society	users.supernet.com/pages/ jdocktor/washmap.htm

| World Atlas | **geography.about.com/library/ maps/blindex.htm** |

World Atlas	**www.sitesatlas.com/**
World Atlas	**thedeejays.com/atlas**
World Maps for Web Sites	**www.theodora.com/maps/new2/ more_world_maps.html**
World Maps from Map Marketing	**www.mapmarketing.com/ indexse.asp**

Information

The world is full of useless information. If you like collecting it, visit some of these sites.

C.E.T. Trivia Quiz	**osiris.sunderland.ac.uk/online/ quiz/quiztime.html**
EastEnders Trivia	**www.walford.net/**
Encarta Quizzes	**encarta.msn.co.uk/quiz/**
Internet Trivia Quiz Directory	**msn.jamba.co.uk/games/trivia/**
Thomas: Legislation Info on the Internet	**thomas.loc.gov/**

Shopping

There are thousands of shopping sites on the Internet which allow you to choose a product and then pay for it online.

Auctions

Selling and buying at an auction is great fun, I'm assured. Using an Internet auction is just as much fun and you can bid across the world. Some auction sites actually own the stock themselves whilst others are merely brokers for third parties to sell.

Able Auctions	**www.ableauctions.com/**
Afternic	**www.afternic.com/**
Allegro Auction	**www.allegro.com.sg/**
Amazon Auctions	**www.amazon.com/**
Antiquorum	**www.antiquorum.com/**
Aucland	**www.aucland.co.uk/**
Auction Addict	**www.auctionaddict.com/**
Auction Classifieds	**www.cityauction.com/**
Auction Depot	**www.auctiondepot.com/**
Auction Guide	**www.auctionguide.com/**

Auction Hunter	www.auctionhunter.com/
Auction IT	www.auction-it.net/
Auction Port	www.auctionport.com/

Auction Watch	www.auctionwatch.com/
Auctionet	www.auctionet.com/
Auction-Land	www.auction-land.com/
Auctionrover	www.auctionrover.com/
Auctions.com	www.auctions.com/
Auctiontrader	www.auctiontrader.com.au/
Auction-Warehouse	www.auction-warehouse.com/
Bestads	www.bestads.com/
Bid Bonanza	www.bidbonanza.com/
Bid Now	www.bidnow.com/
Bid.com	www.bid.com/
BidAway	www.bidaway.com/
Biddington's	www.biddingtons.com/
Bidn4it	www.bidn4it.com/
Blasfer	www.blasfer.com/
Blue Cycle	www.bluecycle.com/
Boston.com	auctions.boston.com/
Boxlot Auction	www.boxlot.com/
Bullnet online auctions	www.bullnet.co.uk/auctions/

Buy Bid Win	www.buybidwin.com/
Buy it	www.buyit.com/
CDSeek	www.cdseek.com/
Collecting Nation	www.collectingnation.com/
Deal Deal	www.dealdeal.com/
DealerNet.com	www.dealernet.com/
Dupont Registry	www.dupontregistry.com/
e Hammer	www.ehammer.com/
Easy Auction	www.easyauction.com/
eBase5	www.ebase5.com/
eBay	www.ebay.com/
eBid	www.ebid.co.uk/
Elance	www.elance.com/
EP	www.ep.com/
Excite Auctions	auctions.excite.com/
Free Forum	www.freeforum.com/
Freemarkets	www.freemarkets.com/
Gavelnet	www.gavelnet.com/

Gibson	www.gibson.com/

Go Ricardo	**www.goricardo.com/**
Grupo Control	**www.grupocontrol.com/**
GunBroker	**www.gunbroker.com/**
Heffel.com	**www.heffel.com/**
Heritage Coin	**www.heritagecoin.com/**
Hobby Markets	**www.hobbymarkets.com/**
Holiday Auctions	**www.holidayauctions.net/**
Honesty	**www.honesty.com/**
iCollector	**www.icollector.com/**

Imandi	**www.imandi.com/**
Infinite Horizon	**www.infinitehorizon.com/auctions.htm**

Interactive Auction Online	www.iaoauction.com/
Internet Auction List	www.internetauctionlist.com/
Jewelnet Auctions	www.jewelnetauctions.com/
Justdeals	www.justdeals.com/
Live Auction Online	www.liveauctiononline.com/
Live to Play	www.livetoplay.com/
London art	www.londonart.co.uk/
Loot	www.loot.com/
Lycos Auctions	auctions.lycos.com/
Meta Exchange	www.metaexchange.com/
Mister Vintage	www.mistervintage.com/
Nationwide Equine Auction	www.equineauction.com/
Net Auction	www.netauction.com/
Onsale Auction Supersite	www.onsale.com/
Polar Auctions	www.polarauctions.com/
Pottery Auction	www.potteryauction.com/
Prints	www.prints.com/
QXL	www.qxl.com/
Rocket8	www.rocket8.com/
Rotman Auction	www.rotmanauction.com/
Sell and Trade	www.sellandtrade.com/
Shopnow	www.shopnow.com/
Sold	www.sold.com.au/
Sporting Auction	www.sportingauction.com/
StampBourse	www.stampbourse.com/

Surplus Auction	www.surplusauction.com/
The American West	theamericanwest.com/
The Thesaurus Group	www.thesaurus.co.uk/
Travelbids	www.travelbids.com/
U Auction it	www.uauction.com/
U Bid 4 it	www.ubid4it.com/
U Bid Online Auction	www.ubid.com/
Up 4 Sale	www.up4sale.com/
URU link	www.urulink.com/
What the heck is that	www.whattheheckisthat.com/
Wine Bid	www.winebid.com/
Yahoo auctions	auctions.yahoo.com/
ZDNet	auctions.zdnet.com/

Shopping Malls

A virtual shopping mall is designed to work in a similar way to a real
shopping mall – the mall itself sells nothing, but houses stores
which do. You can 'walk' through the mall, just as you would in
real life, visit the shops within the mall and buy from any if you
wish. Some malls offer single payment for all purchases, regardless
of which shops you buy from.

@InterMall	iaswww.com/mall
African–American Shopping Mall	www.bnl.com/aasm/
All-Internet Shopping Directory	www.all-internet.com/
Antique Alley	bmark.com/aa

Asian Mall	www.asianmall.com/
Classic England Shopping Mall	www.classicengland.co.uk/
Clothesnet.Com	www.clothesnet.com/
Cowboy Mall	www.cowboymall.com/
Ecomall	www.ecomall.com/
EduMart	www.edumart.com/
eSmarts	www.esmarts.com/
Fashion Mall	www.fashionmall.com/

| Hotnew.com | www.hotnew.com/ |
| International Mall | www.nativecreations.com/ |

NetMarket	www.netmarket.com/
Planet Shopping Network	www.planetshopping.com/
SafeStreet Shopping Centre	www.safestreet.co.uk/
ShopGuide	www.shopguide.com/
Shopping Network	www.planetshopping.com/
Shopping.com	www.shopping.com/ibuy
SkyMall	www.skymall.com/
Spree.com	www.spree.com/
Student Center: Shopping Mall Section	studentcenter.infomall.org/
The Best Mall	www.thebestmall.com/
The Registry	www.thereg.com/
Wineday	www.foodwine.com/food/wineday
Wines on the Internet	www.wines.com/

More Bargains

These sites offer a wide range of products and many of the goods are significantly lower than high street prices.

| Alta Vista | shopping.altavista.com/home.sdc |

| Bigsave.com | **www.bigsave.com/** |
| British Shopping Links | **www.british-shopping.com/** |

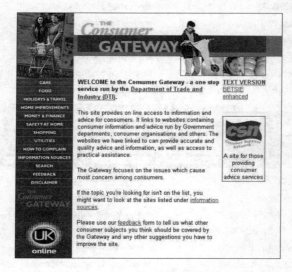

Consumer Gateway	**www.consumer.gov.uk/**
Egg Shopping	**shopping.egg.com/shopping**
Fish4 Online Shopping	**www.fish4.co.uk/category/shopping/**
Freeserve – Shopping	**www.freeserve.com/shopping/**
Gus Home Shopping	**www.gus.co.uk/**
Homefree Shopping	**homefree.co.uk/**

LetsBuyIt.com	www.letsbuyit.com/
Online Shopping UK	www.internetics.co.uk/shop/
Shop Guide	www.shopguide.co.uk/
Shop TV	www.shop-tv.co.uk/
Shop!	www.shop-i.co.uk/
Shopping from Yell	www.shopyell.co.uk/
Shopping On The Net	www.shoppingonthenet.co.uk/
Shopping Unlimited	shoppingunlimited.co.uk/

ShopSmart.com	www.shopsmart.com/
Smartshop	www.smartshop.com/
UK Online Shopping	www.ukonlineshopping.com/
UK Shopping City	www.ukshops.co.uk/
WebMarket	www.webmarket.com/
World of Shopping	www.worldofshopping.com/

Consumer Advice

There are some rogue traders on the Internet, just as there are in everyday life. If you should fall foul of one, get some advice.

| Online Shopping | www.oft.gov.uk/html/shopping/ |
| Which? – Shopping | www.which.net/shopping/
contents.html |

Special Occasions

We all have occasions which are special for one reason or another. The Internet can provide help for all special times.

Birthdays

It happens every year when we begin a new orbit of the sun. If you still feel the need to mark the event, drop hints to friends and family to visit some of these sites.

Astrology Birthday Gifts	www.astrologybirthdaygifts.com/
Birthday Chocolates	www.birthdaychocolates.com/
Birthday Direct	birthdaydirect.com/
Birthday Gifts	www.alltherightgifts.com/ bpbirthday.htm
BK Puff & Stuff	www.bkpuffnstuff.com/
Classique Gifts and Baskets	www.classiquegifts.com/
Fill A Basket	www.fillabasket.com/
First Names	www.firstnames.com/
Gift Idea Center	www.giftideacenter.com/
GiftExpress.com	www.giftexpress.com/

giftwrapgifts.com	www.giftwrapgifts.com/
Happy Birthday Bakery	www.wireacake.com/
iBirthday	www.ibirthday.com/
It Store	www.itstore.com/
Little Birthday Gift	www.shockwave.com/bin/ shockwave/entry.jsp?content =mm20
Make It Personal	www.mipersonal.com/
OvertheHillGifts.com	www.overthehillgifts.com/

Personalized Birthday Gifts	www.personalize.com/

| Sears – Wishbook | www.wishbook.com/ |
| Wonderfully Wacky | www.wonderfullywacky.com/ |

Christmas

12 Days of Christmas Gifts	www.12daysofchristmasgifts.com/
BBC Food at Christmas	www.bbc.co.uk/food/christmas/
BeMe.com – Christmas	www.beme.com/
Cardkingdom.co.uk	www.cardkingdom.co.uk/
Celebrations	www.celebrations-uk.com/
Christmas Gifts	www.christmasgifts.com/
Christmasplace.com	www.ChristmasPlace.com/
ChristmasPresents4u.com	christmaspresents4u.com/
Crocus.co.uk – Christmas	www.crocus.co.uk/christmas/
Family Hampers	www.familyhampers.co.uk/
Gift Warren	www.giftwarren.com/
Gift Time	www.gifttime.co.uk/
Gift Tree	www.gifttree.com/
Gifts to Drink	www.giftstodrink.co.uk/
Goodies	www.interdart.co.uk/goodies/
Happy Christmas.com	www.happychristmas.com/
Highland Fayre	www.highlandfayre.co.uk/
Perfect Present Picker	www.presentpicker.com
PC Advisor – Ultimate Gift Guide	www.pcadvisor.co.uk/news/special/
Sainsbury's Christmas	www.sainsburys.co.uk/christmas/

Shopping Unilimited – Christmas	www.shoppingunlimited.co.uk/ 0,5800,403979,00.html
ShopSmart.com – Christmas	uk.shopsmart.com/Christmas/
Xmas.co.uk	www.xmas.co.uk/

Flowers

Sending flowers is a great way to demonstrate that you are thinking of someone, be it your Mum, spouse or 'friend'. Most of these sites will allow you to order online and specify where they are to be delivered. Some even offer a reminder service which will automatically email you to remind you of an approaching occasion for which flowers would be deemed highly appropriate.

| 101 Flowers | www.101flowers.net/ |

| 1-800 Flowers | www.1800flowers.com/ |
| 1-800 I Love You | www.800iloveyou.com/ |

1-800-SendMaui	www.sendmaui.com/
4Florist	www.4florist.com/
4Flowers	www.4flowers.com/
911Florist	www.911florist.com/
Axelrod and Bennet	www.flowers-florist.com/
Bamboo Green Florist	www.bambooflorist.com.my/
Beautiful Bouquet Florist	www.beautifulbouquet.com/
BestFlowers.com	www.bestflowers.com/
Brecka's Floral and Gifts Company	www.breckasfloral.com/
Calyx and Corolla	www.calyxandcorolla.com/
Cyberflowers	www.cyberflowers.com/
Find Flowers	www.findflowers.com/
Floral Alliance	www.floralalliance.com/
Floresnaweb.com	floresnaweb.com/
Florist Directory	www.florist-directory.com/
Flower Korea	www.flowerkorea.com/
Flowerbud.com	www.flowerbud.com/
Flowers Etc	www.ftd.com/flowers
Flowers NZ	www.downtown.co.nz/flowers-nz/
Flowers: The Shopping Guide	shoppingguide.hypermart.net/flowers.html
Flowers-4-You	www.flowers-4-you.com/index1.htm
Flower Web	www.flowerweb.nl/
Flower Wire	www.flowerwire.com/

Funeral Flowers	www.funeralflowers.com/
Great Flowers	www.greatflowers.com/
Interflora	www.interflora.co.uk/
Israel Flowers	www.flowers.co.il/
Lee Flower	www.leeflower.com/
My Flowers	www.myflowers.com.sg/
My Flowers	www.myflowers.com.my/
National Flora	www.nationalflora.com/
Online Flower Delivery	www.onlineflowerdelivery.net/
Oregon Teleflora Florist	www.flowersoregon.com/
Paul's Flower Shop	www.paulsflower.com/
Princes Flower Shop Pte Ltd	www.prince.com.sg/

proflowers.com
Freshest flowers direct from the grower.

ProFlowers.com	www.proflowers.com/
Russia Florists	www.russiaflorists.com/
Sentiments Express	www.sentiments-express.com/
Spring Bloom	www.madurai.com/class/springbloom
Teleflowers	www.teleflowers.com/
The Florist Directory	www.yourlocalflorist.com/
Wholesale Flowers	www.sdflowers.com/
Worldwide Florist	worldwide-florist.com/

Gifts

It's great to receive presents but it's even better to give. Except that it can take an inordinate amount of time to find and send a present.

Alternative Gift Company	www.alt-gifts.com/
Cardkingdom.co.uk	www.cardkingdom.co.uk/
Country Homes Collectibles & Gifts	www.collectible-gifts.com/
Dial A Basket Gift Service	www.heartphelt.co.uk/
EasyJet Gifts	www.easyjetgifts.com/
Gift Box	www.gotogifts.co.uk/for/silver
Gift Bureau Ideas and Information	www.loud-n-clear.com/gifts
Gift Delivery Company	www.giftdeliveryco.com/
Gift Ideas	www.gotogifts.co.uk/
Gift Selection Online	www.giftselection.co.uk/
Gift Time	www.gifttime.co.uk/
Gifts to Drink	www.giftstodrink.co.uk/
Goodies – Gifts for all Occasions	www.interdart.co.uk/goodies
Internet Gift Store	www.internetgiftstore.com/
Kaven – Essentials for Women	www.gifts-for-women.co.uk/
Lastminute.com Love Gifts	www.lastminute.com/
More Gifts	www.more-gifts.co.uk/
Owl Barn Gift Catalogue	www.the-owl-barn.com/
Promark Business Gifts	www.promark.demon.co.uk/
Quality Gifts	www.quality-gifts.co.uk/

R & D Gifts & Woodcraft	www.gotogifts.co.uk/for/woodcrafts
Scottish Gifts	www.scotch-corner.co.uk/
Star Names	www.starnames.co.uk/
Stork Express Baby Gifts	www.storkexpress.co.uk/
Tartan Gift	www.tartangift.co.uk/
Thorntons Online Store	www.thorntons.co.uk/

Valentine's Day

The day that lovers remember each other seems to take more and more planning each year.

Amore on the Net Valentines Day	www.holidays.net/amore
Blue Mountain Valentines	www1.bluemountain.com/eng/valentine
Confetti Valentines	www.confetti.co.uk/valentines/default.asp
Egreetings – Who do you love?	www.egreetings.com/
Epicurious – Valentine's Day	epicurious.com/e_eating/e04_valentine/valentine.html
Lastminute.com Love Gifts	www.lastminute.com/
Lovingyou.com's Valentine's Day Guide	holidays.lovingyou.com/february
Remember Valentine's Day	orders.mkn.co.uk/valentin/.en
Sugarplums	www.w2.com/docs2/act/food/sugarplums/holidays.html
Valentine's Day Links	orders.mkn.co.uk/valentin/links.en

| Valentine's Love Messages | www.123greetings.com/events/valentinesday |
| Valentines.com | www.valentines.com/ |

Weddings

The day when two people publicly declare their commitment to each other needs to go without a hitch. Whether it be advice, presents, etiquette or hiring the dress, the Internet can help.

Absolutely Wedding Crackers	mkn.co.uk/help/cracker/wedding
Accent Bridal Accessories	www.directproducts.com/accent
Advantage Discount Bridal	www.advantagebridal.com/
BestBridesmaid.com	www.bestbridesmaid.com/
Bridal Creations	www.bridalcreations.com/
Bridal Info	www.bridalinfo.co.uk/
Bridal Marketplace	www.bridalmarketplace.com/
Bridesmaids.com	www.bridesmaids.com/
Chris Peake Wedding Stationery	www.weddingstationery.freeserve.co.uk/
Confetti	www.confetti.co.uk/
Demetrios Wedding Gowns	www.weddingguideuk.com/index.asp
Guild of Wedding Photographers	www.gwp-uk.co.uk/
Romance and Valentino	www.msn.co.uk/page/13-104.asp
Web Wedding	www.webwedding.co.uk/
Wedding Belles	www.wedding-belles.co.uk/
Wedding City	www.wedding-city.co.uk/

Wedding Design Studio	**www.weddingdesignstudio.co.uk/**
Wedding Guide UK	**www.weddingguide.co.uk/**
Wedding Information Service	**www.wedding.demon.co.uk/**
Wedding Jokes	**www.weddingjokes.com/**
Wedding Pages	**www.wedding-pages.co.uk/**
Wedding Present	**www.westnet.com/weddoes/**
Wedding Services	**www.wedding-services.demon.co.uk/**
Wedding Stationery	**www.wedding-stationery.com/**

How to get from here

...to here

THE WEDDING DAY GUIDE

tells you everything... except who to ask

Wedding-day.co.uk	**www.wedding-day.co.uk/**
Weddings & Brides (UK)	**www.weddings-and-brides.co.uk/**
Weddings UK	**www.weddings.co.uk/**

Sport

Sport is probably the most popular free-time pursuit. For every sport you can think off, and most of those you can't, there are dozens of websites produced by both the governing body and by supporters.

Assorted Sports

Most of these sites comment on sport in general although some are dedicated to a specific sport.

AFL	**www.afl.com.au/**
Baseball	**www.baseball.com/**
Biking	**www.bikinguk.net/**
Canoe	**www.canoe.ca/**
CBS SportsLine	**www.sportsline.com/**
CNN – Sports Illustrated	**www.cnnsi.com/**
ESPN.com	**espn.sportszone.com/**
Fogdog	**www.fogdog.com/**
Fox Sports	**www.foxsports.com/**
Headbone	**www.headbone.com/**

LiveScore	www.livescore.com/
Major League Baseball	www.majorleaguebaseball.com/
NBA.com	www.nba.com/
NFL.com	www.nfl.com/

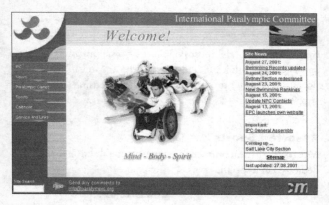

Paralympics	www.paralympic.org/
Sandbox	www.sandbox.com/
Sporting Life	www.sporting-life.com/
Sports	www.sports.com/
Sportstalk	www.sportstalk.com/
That's Racin'	www.thatsracin.com/
The Mountain Zone	www.mountainzone.com/
The Sporting News	www.sportingnews.com/

| The Sports Network | www.sportsnetwork.com/ |
| Times Mirror Interzines | www.tminterzines.com/ |

Extreme Sports

For some people, gentle sports like tiddlywinks are not enough. They need to go bungee-jumping or free-falling out of an aeroplane at 10,000ft with a surfboard.

Adrenaline Sports	www.adren-a-line.com/
Adventure Time Magazine	www.adventuretime.com/
Break the Limits	student.hivolda.no/brandan/sport.htm
Gravity Games	www.gravitygames.com/
Gravity Graphics	gravitygraphics.com/
Motocross	www.motocross.com/
Mountain Zone	www.mountainzone.com/ski/
MX World	www.mxworld.com/
New Zealand Boarder Zone	www.boarderzone.co.nz/
Off-Road	www.off-road.com/
Paraglider	www.poweredparaglider.com/
Pirates of the Rubicon 4WD Club	www.pirate4x4.com/
Sierra Rock Crawlers	www.sierrarockcrawlers.com/
Ski Central	skicentral.com/
Top Rusty Surfboards	www.rusty.com/
Top Skateboard Science	www.exploratorium.edu/skateboarding/

Top Snowboarding Online	**www.twsnow.com/**
Wake World	**www.wakeworld.com/**
Xtreme Scene	**www.xtremescene.com/**

Cricket

There are two sides – one's in the clubhouse, the other's out in the field. The side that's in is out, and the side that's out are trying to get all those in, out. Very confusing.

CricInfo	**www.cricket.org/**
Cricket Direct	**www.cricketdirect.co.uk/**
Cricket Unlimited	**www.cricketunlimited.co.uk/**
Cricket World Monthly	**www.cricketworld.com/**
Cricketer International	**www.cricketer.co.uk/**
Lord's – English & Welsh Cricket Board	**www.lords.org/**
Sky Sports – Cricket	**www.sky.co.uk/sports/cricket/**
Sporting Life – Cricket	**www.sporting-life.com/cricket/ news/**
Women's Cricket Association	**users.ox.ac.uk/~beth/wca.htm**

Equestrian

This is all about trying to steer a horse around a course, of course.

Auckland Show Jumping Group	**www.auckland.jumper.com/**
British Show Jumping Association	**www.bsja.co.uk/**
eQuestrian	**equest.remus.com/**

Jump! Magazine	jumpmagazine.com/
Olympic Games Equestrian Three Day	www.orbital.co.za/olympic/eqsttred.htm
Show Jumping	www.expage.com/page/sj
The Equestrian Times	www.horsenews.com/live/showjump.htm
UAE Equestrian and Racing Federation	www.smartvision.ch/uae/

Football

Bill Shankley once said, "Some people think football is a matter of life and death. They're wrong, it's much more important than that." Nuff said.

BBC Online – Football	www.bbc.co.uk/sport/football/
Daily Soccer	www.dailysoccer.com/
English Football Association	www.the-fa.org/
FIFA.com	www.fifa.com
Football	www.football.smallworld.com/
Football Supporters' Assoc.	www.fsa.org.uk/
Football Unlimited	www.footballunlimited.co.uk/
Football365	www.football365.co.uk/
FootballNews	www.footballnews.co.uk/
Professional Footballers Assoc.	www.thepfa.co.uk/
Sky Sports – Football	www.sky.co.uk/sports/football
Soccernet	www.soccernet.com/
Sportal	www.sportal.co.uk/

The Football League   **www.football-league.co.uk/**
UEFA   **www.uefa.com/**

Formula 1

Isn't it ironic that Formula 1 motor races, with enormously fast and powerful cars, are frequently decided when the cars are in the pits, stationary and on jacks!

Atlas F1	**www.atlasf1.com/**
Autosport	**www.autosport.com/**
Daily F1	**www.dailyf1.com/**
F1 Live	**www.f1-live.com/GB**
F1 Merchandise	**www.f1merchandise.co.uk/**
F1 Online	**www.f1online.de/international**
F1 Picture Net	**www.f1picturenet.com/**
F1 Instinct	**www.f1-instinct.com/**
Formula 1.co.uk	**www.formula-1.co.uk/**
Formula 1.com	**www.formula1.com/**
Formula 1 World	**www.formulaoneworld.co.uk/**
Formula One Supporters Association	**www.fosa.org/**
Gale Force F1	**www.galeforcef1.com/**
Grand Prix History	**www.ddavid.com/formula1**
ITV – Formula One	**www.itv-f1.com/**
Jordan F1	**www.jordangp.com/**
McLaren Magazine	**www.mclaren.co.uk/**

Mercedes-Benz	www.mercedes-benz.com/e/msports/formula1
Sky Sports – Formula One	www.sky.co.uk/sports/center/formula1.htm
Sporting Life – Formula One	www.sporting-life.com/formula1/news/

| Williams F1 | www.williamsf1.co.uk/ |

Golf

A good walk spoiled, until you reach the 19th hole, that is.

| English Golf Union | www.englishgolfunion.org/ |
| Golf History | www.golf-historian.co.uk/ |

Golf Reservations	www.golf-reservations.co.uk/
Golf Today	www.golftoday.co.uk/
Golf UK	www.golfzone.co.uk/
Golf Web	www.golfweb.com/
PGA.com	www.pga.com/
Scottish Golf	www.scottishgolf.com/
Slazenger Golf UK	www.slazengergolf.co.uk/
Sporting Life – Golf	www.sporting-life.com/golf/news/
UK Golf	www.uk-golf.com/

Motor Sport

If it's got more than one wheel, you can bet there is a race somewhere for it.

About.com – Auto Racing	autoracing.about.com/
CART	www.cart.com/
CBS SportsLine – Auto Racing	www.sportsline.com/u/racing/auto/
CNN/SI – Motor Sports	www.cnnsi.com/motorsports
FIA	www.fia.com/
Grassroots Motorsports	www.grmotorsports.com/
Motor Sports Association	www.ukmotorsport.com/racmsa
Motorsport News International	www.motorsport.com/
MotorSports (Bikes)	www.sportbikes.net/
Motorsports Weekly Online	www.motorsportsweekly.com/
NASCAR Online	www.nascar.com/

NHRA Online	www.nhra.com/
North American Motorsport	www.na-motorsports.com/
Race Net International Motorsports	www.nerc.com/~pcs/racenet.html
Race Net International Motorsports	www.tao.com/racenet.html
Rally Zone	www.rallyzone.co.uk/
RSAC – Motor Sport	www.motorsport.co.uk/ rsacms.html
UK Motor Sport Index	www.ukmotorsport.com/

Rugby

This very popular European game is played by 22 men with odd-shaped balls.

Allied Dunbar Premiership Rugby	www.rugbyclub.co.uk/
International Rugby Board	www.irfb.com/
ITV Rugby World Cup	www.itv-rugby.co.uk/
Planet Rugby	www.planetrugby.co.uk/
Rugby Football Union	www.rfu.com/
Rugby Heaven	www.rugbyheaven.com/
Rugby Leaguer	www.rugbyleaguer.co.uk/
Rugby News	www.rugbynews.net/
Scrum.com	www.scrum.com/
Sporting Life – Rugby League	www.sporting-life.com/rleague/ news/

Sporting Life – Rugby Union   **www.sporting-life.com/rugby/
news/**

Snooker

At one stage during the 1980s it seemed that snooker was on every night. You could watch a few frames in one tournament, change channels and see the same players in a different tournament.

Australian Billiards & Snooker   **www.billsnook.com.au/**
Embassy World Snooker   **www.embassysnooker.com/**
Snookernet   **www.snookernet.com/**

Table Tennis

It's always worth seeing the Chinese national team playing Ping-Pong. Do they still throw the ball into the rafters when they serve and hold the bat upside down?

British Olympic Association –   **www.olympics.org.uk/**
Table Tennis   **tabletennis.htm**
Table Tennis   **tabletennis.about.com/**
Table Tennis – USA   **www.usatt.org/**

Tennis

This version of bat 'n' ball (although the 'bat' has become a 'racket') has a huge following and some very skillful players who hand rocket the ball at frightening speeds.

ATP Tour Tennis Online   **www.atptour.com/**

British Olympic Association – Tennis	**www.olympics.org.uk/tennis.htm**
International Tennis Federation	**www.itftennis.com/**
Lawn Tennis Association	**www.lta.org.uk/**
Royal Tennis Court	**www.realtennis.gbrit.com/**
Sky Sports – Tennis	**www.sky.co.uk/sports/tennis/**
Sporting Life – Tennis	**www.sporting-life.com/tennis/news/**
Tennis Net	**www.btinternet.com/~tennis.net/**
Tennis Wales	**www.tennis.wales.org/**
Tennis Worldwide Chat	**www.tennisw.com/chat.html**

Wimbledon.com	**www.wimbledon.com/**

Wrestling

Once the preserve of the Saturday afternoon TV sports show, the participants never seemed to have much regard for the rules, and the referee didn't seem to be able to do much about it. Now it's undergone a re-birth, there seems even less regard for rules and absolutely no consideration to fair play.

BAWA	www.homeusers.prestel.co.uk/bawa/
British Internet Wrestling Federation UK	members.xoom.com/biwf
British Wrestling	www.britishwrestling.cwc.net/
Calendar of Wrestling Events	home.clara.net/pb
Freestyle Wrestling	www.dcs.shef.ac.uk/~mlee/social/wrestling.html
NWA-UK Hammerlock Wrestling	www.hammerlock-wrestling.com/
Official Women of Wrestling	www.owow.com/
Scoop's Wrestling Fan's Network	www.scoopscentral.com/
WCW	www.wcw.com/
World Championship Wrestling	www.wcwwrestling.com/
World of Wrestling	www.worldofwrestling.co.uk/
World Wrestling Federation	www.wwf.com/
Wrasslin	www.wrasslin.com/
Wrestle Line	www.wrestleline.com/
Wrestling Online	www.stbarnabas.demon.co.uk/
Wrestling.com	www.1wrestling.com/

Technology

During the last 50 years there has been a headlong rush of new sophisticated technology that previously couldn't even have been dreamed about. What is more incredible is that this technology is affordable by almost everyone.

Cameras and Photography

I've never owned a good camera other than a digital one. The reason is that when I embark on something new I like to do it wholly. That would mean a darkroom, developing equipment and all the paraphernalia that goes with it. I've never had the space to get into that. One day maybe.

1st Cameras	www.1stcameras.co.uk/
20-20Consumer	www.20-20consumer.com/
4 Cameras	www.4cameras.com/
888-camcorder	www.888camcorder.com/
AAA Camera	www.aaacamera.com/
AAAnet	www.aaanet-inc.com/
Abbey Camera	abbeycamera.com/

Abe's Of Maine	www.abesofmaine.com/
Abes Camera and Video	www.abescamera.com/
Abolins Inc	www.abolins.com/
Access Cameras and Film	www.123-cameras.com/
Access Discount Camera	www.accesscamera.com/
Adolph Gasser Inc	www.gassers.com/
Adorama Camera	www.adorama.net/
Amazing Holga	www.holgacamera.com/
Apex Photo	www.apexphoto.net/
Apogee Photography Guide	www.apogeephoto.com/
Art's Cameras Plus	www.artscamera.com/
B&H Photo-Video-Pro Audio	www.bhphotovideo.com/
Beach Camera	beachcamera.com/
Beach Photo and Video	beachphoto.com/
Bel Air Camera	www.belaircam.com/
Bender Photographic Inc	www.benderphoto.com/
Best Photo Video	www.bestphotovideo.com/
Bob Davis Camera	www.bobdaviscamera.com/
Bridge Net	www.bridgenet.com.tw/
Broadway Camera	www.broadwaycamera.com/
Calumet Photographic	www.calumetphoto.com/
Cambridge Camera Exchange	www.cambridgeworld.com/
Camera Corner	www.camcor.com/
Camera Craft Shop Online	www.cameracraft.com/
Camera Depot	www.cameradepot.co.uk/

Camera Direct	www.camera-direct.com/
Camera House	www.camerahouse.com.au/
Camera People	www.camerapeople.net/
Camera Store	www.camerastore.com.au/
Camera Store	www.thecamerastore.net/
Cameras Brookwood	www.camerasbrookwood.com/
Cameras Direct	www.camerasdirect.co.uk/
Cameraworld.com	www.cameraworld.com/
Charlotte Camera	charlottecamera.com/
CoCam Photo	www.cocam.co.uk/
Community Camera Center	www.communitycamera.com/
D.L. Accents	www.dlaccents.com/
Dale Photographic Services	www.dalephotographic.co.uk/
Dan's Camera City	www.danscamera.com/
Digital Distributors	www.digitaletc.com/
Discount Camera	www.discountcamera.com/
E.P.Levine Inc	www.cameras.com/
Eaglecameraone.com	www.eaglecameraone.com/
European Camera Specialists	sites.netscape.net/eurocameras/
F/Stop Camera Corporation	www.f-stopcamera.com/
Ffordes Photographic Ltd	www.ffordes.co.uk/
Fife Foto Centre	www.fifefotocentre.co.uk/
Flashcube	www.flashcube.com/
Ginfax Development Limited	www.ginfax.com/
Glazer's Camera Supply	www.glazerscamera.com/

Goodwin Photo Inc	www.goodwinphotoinc.com/
Harry Pro Shop	harrysproshop.com/
Harvard Camera	www.harvardcamera.com/
Hawaiian Camera Supply	www.hassy.com/
Henry's Cameras and Electronics	www.henrys.com/
Igor's Camera Exchange	www.igorcamera.com/
JCR Cameras	www.jcr-cameras.com/
Jens Madsen Cameras and Imaging	www.madsens.com.au/

Jessops	www.jessops.com/
Karl Heitz Service	www.karlheitz.com/
Kenmore Camera	www.kcamera.com/
Leica Store	www.theleicastore.com/
Lotts Photo	www.lottsphoto.com/

LR Mansley Ltd	www.camera-centre.co.uk/
Lumière Shop	www.fotolaborgeraete.de/
Main Street	www.ashlandcamera.com/
McRill's Cameras	www.cameraguy.com/
Morris Photographic Centre	www.morrisphoto.co.uk/
Nat. Camera and Video Exchange	www.nationalcamera.com/
Northern Photographics	www.northernphotographics.com/
Oakdale-Bohemia Camera Inc	www.obcameras.com/
Patience Photographic Co Ltd	www.patience-photographic.co.uk/
Photo Alley	www.photoalley.com/
Photo Factory	www.photofactory.com.au/
Photo Shopping Guide	www.photomagazines.com/
Photo Source	www.mmphoto.com/
Photoco	www.photococan.com/
Photographx Unlimited	www.photographxunlimited.com/
Photomall.com	www.photomall.com/
Photorama	www.photorama.com/
Photoshopper	www.photoshopper.com/
Porter's Camera Store	www.porters.com/
Precision Camera and Video	www.precision-camera.com/
Prime Direct	www.primedirect.com/
ProCam Online	www.procam.com/
Ritz Camera Centers	www.ritzcamera.com/
Roberts Imaging	www.robertsimaging.com/

Russian Camera Exchange	www.gkweb.com/rcx/
Studio Outlet	www.studio-outlet.com/
Sussex Camera Centre	www.tradecameras.co.uk/
Technik Camera	www.technikcamera.com/
Terry's Camera	www.terryscamera.com/
Thompson Photo Products	www.thompsonphoto.com/
Travel Guides for Photographers	phototravel.com/
UK Camera Shops	www.ukcamera.co.uk/
Unique Photo	www.netphotostore.com/
Unruh Photography Shop	www.flashcube.com/
Vistek	www.vistek.net/
Wall Street Camera	www.wallstreetcamera.com/
Warehouse Photographic	www.warehousephoto.com/
Wolf Camera	www.wolfcamera.com/
Wolfe's	www.wolfes.com/
WolfXpress	www.wolfxpress.com/
World Wide Camera	www.worldwidecamera.com/

Consumer Electronics

There is a bewildering array of HiFi, TV and VCR readily available from countless outlets. Use the Internet to compare different models before buying.

1 Cache	www.1cache.com/
220 volt appliances	www.astrointl.com/
42 St. Photo	www.42photo.com/

4Electronics	www.4electronics.com/
800.com	www.800.com/
A Plus Digital	www.aplusdigital.com/
AAA price	aaaprice.com/
ABT Electronics	www.abtelectronics.com/
Access Electronics	www.123-electronics.com/
Adabra	www.adabra.com/
ALightning Audio Video	www.lightav.com/
Audio Warehouse Express	www.audio-warehouse.com/
Barrel of Monkeys	www.barrel-of-monkeys.com/
Best Buy Co Inc	www.bestbuy.com/
Best Stuff	www.beststuff.co.uk/
BestPriceAudioVideo.com	www.bestpriceaudiovideo.com/
Big Apple Company	www.bigapplecompany.com/
BrandNamez.com	www.brandnamez.com/
Budget HiFi.com	www.budgethifi.com/
Burke's TV Sales	www.burkestv.com/
Buy and More	buyandmore.com/
Buypath	www.buypath.com/electronics
Camcorders 4 sale	www.camcorders4sale.com/
Cheetah Deals	www.cdeals.com/
Circuit City Stores	www.circuitcity.com/
Comet	www.comet.co.uk/
Consumer Direct Online	www.consumerdirectonline.com/
Consumer Direct Warehouse	www.consumer-direct.com/

Crazy Eddie	www.crazyeddieonline.com/
Crazy Electric	www.crazyelectric.com/
Creative.com	www.hifi.com/
Dixons	www.dixons.co.uk/
Earthstations.com	www.earthstations.com/

Electro Buy	www.1-800-electro.com/
Electroland	www.electroland.com/
Electronic Explosion	www.electronicexplosion.com/
Electronic Express	www.electronicexpress.com/
Electronic Zone	www.electronic-zone.com/
Electronicaccessory.com	www.electronicaccessory.com/

Electronic Paradise	www.electronicparadise.com/
Electronics.net	electronics.net/
Electronics4Sale	www.electronics4sale.com/
Electronicsgallery.com	www.electronicsgallery.com/
Etronixs.com	www.etronixs.com/
Everyday Comfort	www.everydaycomfort.com/
e-Widgets.com	www.e-widgets.com/
Export Masters	emcdepot.com/
EZ Electronics	www.ez.com/
Firebox	www.firebox.com/
Future Shop Canada	www.futureshop.ca/
G&G Electronics	ggelectronics.com/
Global Mart	www.globe-mart.com/
Goodguys	www.thegoodguys.com/
Goody Gadgets	www.goodygadgets.com/

Helpful Home Shopping Co	www.helpful.co.uk/

HiFi Buys	www.hifibuys.com/
HomeTicket.com	www.hometicket.com/
IBS Electronics	www.ibsstore.com/
Internet Ontime.com	www.internetontime.com/
J&R Music and Computer World	www.jandr.com/
Lee Electronics	www.leeselect.com/
Luketech	buy.at/luketech
McNo Ltd	www.mcno.com/
MsMart.com	www.msmart.com/
Netmarket	www.netmarket.com/
NextPurchase.Com	www.nextpurchase.com/
Nu-Visions Appliance Co.	www.nu-visions.com/
One Stop Home Technologies	www.osht.com/
Pace Electronics	www.paceworld.com/main.htm
Panasonic Family Dealer	www.panwebi.com/
PCseller.com	www.pcseller.com/
Planet3000	www.planet3000.com/
Powerhouse	www.powerhouse-online.co.uk/
Primefocus.com	www.primefocus.com/
ProActive Electronics	www.proactiveelectronics.com/
QVC	www.qvc.com/
Radio Shack	www.radioshack.com/
RCA	www.rca.com/
Remote controls	www.remotecontrols.co.uk/
Sales Circular.com	www.salescircular.com/

Sony Corp	www.sony.com/
Sound Advice	www.wegivesoundadvice.com/
Sound City Electronics	www.soundcitycorp.com/
Southern Advantage	www.soadv.com/
Spider Gear	www.spidergear.com/
Spiegel Tronics	www.spiegel.com/spiegel/shopping/tronics
Supreme Video & Electronics	www.supremevideo.com/
SutterTel.Com	www.suttertel.com/
Tempo	www.tempo.co.uk/
The Video Doctor II	www.thevideodoctor.com/
Turbo Price	www.turboprice.com/
Tweeter etc.	www.tweeter.com/
Unbeatable	www.unbeatable.co.uk/
Ugonet Photo and Electronics	www.ugonet.com/
Valco Electronics	www.valcoelectronics.com/
Value Direct	www.value-direct.co.uk/
Wacko Deals	www.wackodeals.com/
Watchman Electronics Products	www.watchmanproducts.com/
Web Electricals	www.webelectricals.co.uk/
Wholesale Connection	www.wholesaleconnection.com/
Wholesale Electronics	www.electronicgear.com/
Wholesale Products	www.wholesaleproducts.com/
Worldwide Electronics	www.welectronics.com/

Mobile Phones

I'm not convinced that 90% of the people who own a mobile phone actually need one or even use one enough to justify its cost. Mobile phones are, in fact, little more than fashion accessories but why should I complain. The more people that buy them, the cheaper they become.

Access Telephones and Pagers	www.123-phones.com/
Carphone Warehouse	www.carphonewarehouse.com/
Ham Mall Amateur Radio	www.hammall.com/
Hello Direct.com	www.hellodirect.com/
Independent Technologies	www.independenttech.com/

Mobile Fun   www.mobilefun.co.uk/

Mobile Melodies	www.mobile-melodies.com/
Mobile Phone Store	www.themobilephonestore.com/
Mobiles Phones	www.buy.co.uk/moneysm/ mobiles.asp
Mobilize Now	www.mobilizenow.com/
National Cell Phone Rentals	www.dwellings.com/cell
Nokia	www.nokia.com/
Pocket Phone Shop	www.pocketphone.co.uk/
Phone Center	www.aphone.com/
Phonecity	www.phonecity.co.uk/
Phonethings.com	www.phonethings.com/
Point.com	www.point.com/
Portable Concepts	portableconcepts.com/
Prime Page & Cellular	primepage.net/
Quantometrix	www.quantometrix.com/ Ultim_Lis.htm
Radios Plus.com	radiosplus.com/
Ringtones Direct	www.ringtones-direct.com/
Roy's Phones	www.roysphones.com/
SamsonWeb eStore	www.samsonweb.com/estore
Satellite Warehouse	www.satphone.net/
Sezz	www.sezz.at/
Shop Cordless	www.shopcordless.com/
Shop Wireless	www.shopwireless.com/
Smart Hook	www.singnet.com.sg/~smarthk
Sundial.com	www.sundial.com/

SWS Communications	www.swscommunications.com/
TeleCell	www.telecell.com/
Telephone Superstore	www.telephonesuperstore.com/
The Phone Source	www.thephonesource.com/

The Pocket Phone Shop	www.pocketphone.co.uk/
Ultra Phones	www.ultraphones.com/
World of Wireless	www.worldofwireless.com/

Travel

The Internet is a great way to book travel and holiday accommodation.

Airlines

Every airline has a website and many will allow you to book flights online. Look out for special bargains and take note of airport information including departure and arrival times.

AB Airlines	www.abairlines.com/
Aces Columbia Airlines	www.acescolombia.com/
Aer Lingus	www.aerlingus.ie/
Aeroflot	www.aeroflot.com/
Aerolineas Argentinas	www.aerolineas.com.ar/
Air 2000	www.air2000.co.uk/
Air Atlanta Icelandic	www.airatlanta.com/
Air Baltic	www.airbaltic.lv/
Air Caledonie	www.air-caledonie.nc/
Air Canada	www.aircanada.ca/
Air Europa	www.air-europa.com/

Air Fiji	**airfiji.net/**
Air France	**www.airfrance.com/**
Air India	**www.airindia.com/**
Air Jamaica	**www.airjamaica.com/**
Air Macau	**www.airmacau.com.mo/**
Air Malta	**www.airmalta.com/**
Air Mauritius	**www.airmauritius.com/**
Air Moldova International	**www.ami.md/**
Air Nauru	**www.airnauru.com.au/**

| Air New Zealand | **www.airnewzealand.co.nz/** |
| Air Niugini | **www.airniugini.com.pg/** |

Air Philippines	**airphilippines.com/**
Aircalin	**www.aircalin.nc/**
Airlink	**www.airlink.com.pg/**
Airtours	**www.airtours.com/**
Alaska Airlines & Horizon Air	**www.alaska-air.com/**
Alitalia	**www.alitalia.it/**
All Nippon Airways	**www.ana.co.jp/index_e.html**
Aloha Air	**www.alohaair.com/**
America Trans Air (ATA)	**www.ata.com/**
American Airlines	**www.aa.com/**
American Airlines & American Eagle	**www.americanair.com/**
American World Airways	**welcome.to/ americanworldairways**
Ansett Australia	**www.ansett.com.au/**
Ansett New Zealand	**www.ansett.co.nz/**
Atlantic Airways	**www.atlantic.fo/**
Atlantic Coast Airlines	**www.atlanticcoast.com/**
Austrian Airlines	**www.aua.com/**
Balkan Airlines	**www.balkan.com/**
Baltia Air Lines Inc	**www.iblf.com/baltia.htm**
Belau Air	**www.belauair.com/**
Britannia Airways	**www.britanniaairways.com/**
British Airways	**www.british-airways.com/**
British Midland	**www.iflybritishmidland.com/**
British Regional Airlines Limited	**www.british-regional.com/**

Canadian Airlines International	www.cdnair.ca/
Carnival Airlines	www.carnivalair.com/
Cathay Pacific	www.cathaypacific-air.com/
Cayman Airways	www.caymans.com/caymans/ cayman_airways.html
China Airlines	www.china-airlines.com/
Continental Airlines	www.continental.com/
Cubana Air	www.cubana.cu/index.html
Cyprus Airways	www.cyprusair.com.cy/
Delta Air Lines	www.delta-air.com/index.html
Delta Express	www.delta-air.com/express/ index.html
Dragon Air	www.dragonair.com/
EasyJet	www.easyjet.com/
Finnair	www.finnair.com/
First Air	www.firstair.ca/
Flight West Airlines	www.fltwest.com.au/
Go	www.go-fly.com/
Hawaiian Airlines	www.hawaiianair.com/
Iberia Airlines	www.iberia.com/
Icelandair	www.icelandair.net/
JAL Japan Airlines	www.jal.co.jp/english/ index_e.html
JAT Yugoslav Airlines	www.monarch-airlines.com/
KLM UK	www.klmuk.com/
Korean Air	www.koreanair.com/

Lufthansa InfoFlyway	www.lufthansa.co.uk/
Malaysia Air	www.malaysiaair.com/
Manx Airlines	www.manx-airlines.com/
Mexicana Airlines	www.mexicana.com/index.html
Midway Airlines	www.midwayair.com/
Midwest Express Airlines	www.midwestexpress.com/
Monarch Airlines	www.monarch-airlines.com/
National Airlines	www.nationalairlines.com/
Necon Air	www.neconair.com/
Olympic Airways	www.olympic-airways.gr/
Orient Avia Airlines	www.russia.net/
Pacific Coastal Airlines	www.pacific-coastal.com/
Pacific Wings Hawaii	www.pacificwings.com/
Polynesian Airlines	www.polynesianairlines.co.nz/
Qantas Airlines	www.qantas.com.au/
Ryanair	www.ryanair.ie/
Sahara Airlines	www.saharaairline.com/
Scandinavian Airlines – SAS	www.sas.se/
Shuttle America	www.shuttleamerica.com/
Singapore Airlines	www.singaporeair.com/
Skyways	www.skyways.se/
Skywest Airlines	www.skywest.com.au/
Sobelair	www.sobelair.com/
Solomon Airlines	www.solomonairlines.com.au/
Southern Australia Airlines	www.qantas.com.au/southern/index.html

Southwest Airlines	**www.iflyswa.com/**
Spanair	**www.spanair.com/**
Spirit Airlines	**www.spiritair.com/**
Star Airlines	**www.star-airlines.fr/**
SwissAir	**www.swissair.com/**
SwissJet USA	**swissjet.com/**
Thai Airways International	**www.thaiair.com/**
Trans States Airlines	**www.transstates.net/**
TransBrasil	**www.transbrasil.com.br/**
Transmeridian Airlines	**www.transmeridian-airlines.com/**
TransWorld Airlines	**www.twa.com/**
Turkish Airlines	**www.turkishairlines.com/**
United Airlines	**www.ual.com/**
US Airways	**www.usairways.com/**
VARIG Airlines	**www.varig.com.br/**
VASP Airlines	**www.vasp.com.br/**

Virgin Atlantic UK	**www.virgin-atlantic.com/**
Volare Airlines	**www.volare-airlines.com/**
Vulcanair	**www.vulcanair.com/**
World Airways	**www.worldair.com/**
Yugoslav Airlines	**www.jat.com/**

Cheap/Late Flights

If you like booking at the last minute, or you just seem to end up booking at the last minute, try one of these sites to book a late flight. You can also book economy airfares through these sites.

Air Ticket Centre	www.airticketcentre.co.uk/
Bargain flights.com	www.bargainflights.com/
Bargain holidays.com	www.bargainholidays.com/
Cheap Flights	www.cheapflights.co.uk/
Deckchair.com	www.deckchair.com/
Discount Airfares	www.etn.nl/discount
Discount Holidays Flights	www.dhf.co.uk/
Flight Bookers	www.flightbookers.co.uk/

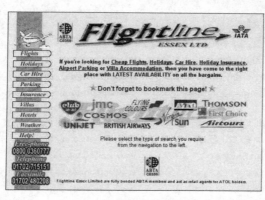

Flight Line	www.flightline.co.uk/

Last Minute	www.lastminute.com/
Netflights	www.netflights.com/
Web Holidays UK	www.webholidays.co.uk/

Boats

The alternative to an aeroplane is a boat, either a cruise liner or a ferry to get you across a particular stretch of water.

| Adventuress River Cruises | rivercruises.co.uk/ |
| Atlantis Cruising | www.atlantistravel.co.uk/ |

Chancery Cruising	www.holborn-travel.co.uk/
Cruise Holidays	www.travelogue.co.uk/
Cruise Transfers	www.airport-transfers-uk.com/cruises.html
Festival Cruises	www.festival.gr/
Fred Olsen Cruise Lines	www.gbnet.co.uk/fred.olsen/
Jacobite Cruises	www.cali.co.uk/jacobite/
Let's Cruise	www.letscruise.co.uk/
P&O Cruises	www.pocruises.com/
Royal Caribbean International	www.rccl.com/

SeaView Cruise & Ferry Information	www.seaview.co.uk/
Swan Hellenic	www.swan-hellenic.co.uk/
The Cruise People	members.aol.com/cruiseaz

Car Hire

Once you've arrived at your destination, you may need to book a car to enable to explore further afield than the airport or ferry terminal.

A One Rent-A-Car	www.aonerentacar.com/
Ace Rent-A-Car	www.acerentacar.com/
Advantage Rent-A-Car	www.arac.com/
Autolease Rent-a-Car	www.autolease-uae.com/
Automotive Resources International	www.arifleet.com/
AutoNet International	www.autonet-intl.com/
Avcar Rental	www.avcar.com/
Avis Rent A Car	www.avis.com/
Beverly Hills Rent-A-Car	www.bhrentacar.com/
BreezeNet's Rental Car Guide	www.bnm.com/miam.htm
British Car Rental	www.bcvr.co.uk/
Crete Car Hire	www.kalithea.demon.co.uk/
Eagle Rent A Car	www.eagle-rent-a-car.com/
Enterprise Rent-A-Car Co.	www.pickenterprise.com/
Eurodrive Car Rental	www.eurodrive.com/

Europa Rent-A-Car	www.intercom.es/eurorent
Europcar	www.europcar.com/
Eurostyle	www.eurostyle.uk.com/
Excellent Car Rental	www.arweb.com/excellent
Heiser Auto Group	www.heiser.com/
Hertz Rent A Car	www.hertz.com/
Holiday Cars Direct	www.holidaycarsdirect.com/
Kemwel Holiday Autos	www.kemwel.com/
Lowestfare.com	www.lowestfare.com/
National Car Rental	www.nationalcar-europe.com/
National Car Rental	www.nationalcar.com/servlet/dochandler/
Payless Car Rental	www.paylesscar.com/
Pegasus Rental Cars	www.rentalcars.co.nz/
Practical Car & Van Rental	www.tsnxt.co.uk/practical/
Rent A Car UK	www.rentacar-uk.com/
Rent A Wreck	www.rent-a-wreck.com/
Rental Car Guide	www.bnm.com/la.htm
Specialty Car Rentals	www.specialtyrentals.com/
Sun Cars	ds.dial.pipex.com/air-flights/
Thrifty Car Rental	www.thrifty.co.uk/
Trip.com	www.thetrip.com/
Vancouver's Lo-Cost Car Rental	www.locost.com/westcoastvan
Woods Car Rental	www.woods.co.uk/

Coaches

If you want to take it slowly, and take in the scenery en route, try a coach. It's frequently the cheapest way to travel.

Astarea	**www.astarea.hr/**
Buses By Bill	**www.buscharters.net/**
Diethelm Travel	**www.diethelm-travel.com/**
Eavesway Travel	**www.eaveswaytravel.com/**
Evan Evans	**www.evanevans.co.uk/**
Globe Treks	**www.globetreks.com/**
Irish Travel	**www.irishtravel.com.au/**
Luxury Travel Motor Coaches	**www.luxurytravelcoaches.com/**
Mayflower Acme Tours	**www.mayflower.com.my/**

National Express	**www.gobycoach.com/**
Nor-Way Bussekspress AS	**www.nbe.no/**
Nova Travel	**www.sleepercoaches.co.uk/**
Putnik Yugoslavia	**www.putnik.co.yu/**
Redwing	**www.redwing-coaches.co.uk/**
Scottish Highlands Travel	**www.host.co.uk/allareas/travel**
Selwyns Travel UK	**www.selwyns.co.uk/**
Sheppard Touring	**sheppard.touring.co.nz/**
Utopia Tours	**www.utopiatours.com/**

Trains

A train journey is generally the fastest way to move overland. It's safe and relatively cheap. These sites have information for tourists including timetables and prices. Some will allow you to book online.

Alaska Railroad	www.akrr.com/
Amtrak	www.amtrak.com/
Association of American Railroads	www.aar.org/
BritRail	www.britrail.co.uk/
Burlington Northern Santa Fe	www.bnsf.com/
Central Trains	users.aol.com/walesrails/ct.htm
CSX Transportation	www.csxt.com/
Delayed.net	www.delayed.net/
Deutsche Bahn AG	www.bahn.de/home_e/f-engl.htm
Eurostar Passenger Services	www.railpass.com/eurostar/
First Great Western	www.great-western-trains.co.uk/
Great Eastern Railway	www.ger.co.uk/
Great Little Trains of Wales	www.whr.co.uk/gltw/
Japan Railway	www.ejrcf.or.jp/
Llangollen Railway	www.marl.com/lds/Lr/llan-railway.html
Midland Mainline	www.midlandmainline.com/
National Rail Corporation	www.nationalrail.com.au/
North Western Trains	nwt.rail.co.uk/

Pikes Peak Cog Railway	www.cograilway.com/
Public Transit in British Columbia	www.transitbc.com/
Queen of Scots	www.queenofscots.co.uk/
Rail Info	www.railinfo.freeserve.co.uk/
Railtrack: Travel Information	www.railtrack.co.uk/
Railway Exchange	www.railwayex.com/
Russian Rail	www.russia-rail.com/
Sightseeing Trains	www.redtrains.com/
Snowdon Mountain Railway	www.snowdonrailway.force9.co.uk/
South West Trains	www.swtrains.co.uk/
Steam Safaris	www.steam-in-south-africa.com/
Thames Trains	www.thamestrains.co.uk/
ThamesLink	www.thameslink.co.uk/
TheTrainline.com	www.thetrainline.com/
Train Hoppers	www.catalog.com/hop
Train-net.co.uk	www.train-net.co.uk/
TrainWeb	www.trainweb.com/
Trans-Siberian Railroad	www.ego.net/tlogue/xsib/
Tranz Rail	www.tranzrail.co.nz/
UK Railways	www.rail.co.uk/
Union Pacific Corporation	www.up.com/
Union Pacific Railroad	www.uprr.com/
Virgin Trains	www.virgintrains.co.uk/
West Coast Railway	www.wcr.com.au/

Holidays

Some people prefer the 'all-in-one' approach and book a holiday that includes travel, accommodation, meals and even excursions.

A Travel Depot	www.atraveldepot.com/
Aerojets	www.web-tech.co.uk/aerojets
B&B	www.beduk.co.uk/
Bargain Holidays	www.bargainholidays.com/
Chez Nous	www.cheznous.com/
Columbus Direct	www.columbusdirect.com/
Cornish Cottages	www.corncott.com/
Corsican Holidays	www.corsica.co.uk/
Country Holidays	www.country-holidays.co.uk/
eBookers.com	www.ebookers.com/
Escape Routes	www.escaperoutes.com/
Happy Time Tours and Travel	www.httours.com/
Internet Holidays	www.holiday.co.uk/
Internet Travel Services	www.its.net/
Ireland Travel	www.12travel.com/
James Villas	www.jamesvillas.com/
Jardine Travel Limited	www.jardine-travel.com.hk/
Last Stop	www.laststop.co.uk/
Magic Travel	www.magictravelgroup.co.uk/
Saga Holidays	www.saga.co.uk/
Scottish Travel	www.travelscotland.co.uk/

Simply Travel	www.simply-travel.com/
Thomas Cook	www.thomascook.com/
Tickets Anywhere	www.ticketsanywhere.co.uk/
Travel Bug	www.flynow.com/
Travel Bug	www.travel-bug.co.uk/
Travel Select	www.travelselect.com/
Travel Travel	www.travel-travel.co.uk/
Travelstore.com	www.travelstore.com/
UK Hotels	www.travellerschoice.net/
Westravel	www.westravel.co.uk/
Worldtravelcenter.com	www.worldtravelcenter.com/

Hotels

If you want to stop over for a night or two, or for whole weeks, there are lots of hotels on the web, many of which can be booked online, or reserved and confirmed by email.

A thru Z Hotel Finder	www.from-a-z.com/
All Hotels on the Web	www.all-hotels.com/
Best Hotel & Inn	www.best-hotel.co.uk/
Blackpool Hotels Directory	www.blackpool-hotels.co.uk/
British Hotel Reservation Centre	www.bhrc.co.uk/
Country House Hotels Great Britain	www.country-house-hotels.com/
Creditview Bed and Breakfast	www.bbcanada.com/
Elegant English Hotels	www.eeh.co.uk/

Everybody's Hotel Directory	www.everybody.co.uk/
Expotel	www.expotel.co.uk/
Firmdale Hotels	www.firmdale.com/
Fodor's Hotel Index: London	www.fodors.com/
Forte Hotels	www.forte-hotels.com/
Headwaters Hideaway Bed and Breakfast	www.bbcanada.com/2121.html
Holiday Inn London	www.bookings.org/uk/html/30072.html
Holiday Inns UK	www.holidayinns.co.uk/
Holiday Inns Worldwide	www.basshotels.com/holiday-inn/
Hotel Guide	www.hotelguide.com/
Hotels & Travel in the UK	www.hotelstravel.com/uk.html
Hotels Etcetera	www.hotelsetc.com/
Jarvis Hotels	www.jarvis.co.uk/
London Hotels	www.demon.co.uk/hotel-net/hotel.html
London Hotels	www.hotelsengland.com/
Morton Hotels	www.morton-hotels.com/
Paramount Hotel Group	www.paramount-hotels.co.uk/
Posthouse Hotels	www.posthouse-hotels.co.uk/
Royal Glenn Hotel	www.blackpool-hotels.com/
Scenic Bed-and-Breakfast	www.bbcanada.com/
Scotland Hotels & Visitor Attractions	www.freedomglen.co.uk/
Smooth Hound: Hotels & Guesthouses	www.s-h-systems.co.uk/

Thistle Hotels   www.thistlehotels.com/

Site of the Month - *Total Internet, volume one, issue three*

One of the largest known UK Hotel and Guest House directories featuring over 10,000 places to stay, many offering exclusive **Smooth Hound** discounts.

We are Britain's leading guide, with a wide range of holiday and business accommodation. Bed & breakfast room rates to suit all pockets. We are easy to use and quick to download, with clickable maps to travel instantly throughout England, Scotland and Wales. Our listings provide comprehensive details of facilities offered, including AA, RAC and Tourist board ratings.

Check us first for exclusive Smooth Hound discounts before booking anywhere in the United Kingdom. Why not bookmark us now!

Click on the map in the area of your choice or select from the list below.

UK Hotels & Guest Houses   www.smoothhound.co.uk/
Virtual Hotels   www.virtualhotels.com/

Maps/Route Instructions

If you're touring the countryside you'll need to know where you're going and how to get there. These map sites should be very useful, especially if you can access the sites whilst you're on the move.

Automobile Association   www.theaa.co.uk/
Digital City   home.digitalcity.com/maps
EuroShell Route Planner   www.shell.com/
Michelin – Route Planner,   www.viamichelin.com/
Hotels and Restaurants

RAC	www.rac.co.uk/
Railroad, Subway and Tram Maps	pavel.physics.sunysb.edu/RR/maps.html
United Kingdom Hotels & Maps	www.guestaccom.co.uk/mapuk.htm

Travel Insurance

Insurance is something we all hope will never be needed, but accidents and mishaps do happen. If you arrive in San Fransisco and your baggage arrives in New York it will be reasurring to know that someone else can have the hassle while you just enjoy yourself.

1st Quote	www.1stquote.co.uk/
A1 Insurance	www.a1insurance.co.uk/
Bellevue Insurance	www.bellevue-ins.co.uk/
CGU Direct	www.cgu-direct.co.uk/
Churchill Insurance	www.churchill.co.uk/
Clover Insurance	www.clover-insurance.demon.co.uk/
Columbus Direct Travel Insurance	www.columbusdirect.co.uk/
Cornhill	www.cornhill.co.uk/
Coversure	www.coversure.co.uk/
CSA Travel Protection	www.travelsecure.com/
Direct Insurance Group	www.digs.co.uk/
Eagle Star Direct	www.eaglestardirect.co.uk/
Endsleigh	www.endsleigh.co.uk/protection/

Global Travel Insurance	www.globalholidays.co.uk/intro.htm
Halifax Travel	www.halifax.co.uk/halifax-travel/
Hamilton Fraser Insurance	www.hamiltonfraser.co.uk/
Hogg Robinson plc	www.hoggrobinson.com/
III Insurance Centre	www.iii.co.uk/insurance/
Insbuyer.com – Travel Insurance	www.insbuyer.com/travelinsurance.htm
Insurance Centre	www.theinsurancecentre.co.uk/
Insurance Wide.com	www.insurancewide.com/
Insure Travel	www.insuretravel.com/
International Student Travel Confederation	www.istc.org/
Jacksons Insurance	www.jacksons-insure.demon.co.uk/
Leading Edge	www.leadedge.co.uk/
Livingstones Insurance	www.livingstones-insurance.co.uk/
Lombard Insurance Brokers Ltd	www.lombardinsurance.co.uk/
Royal & Sun Alliance Insurance	www.royal-and-sunalliance.com/
Saga	www.saga.co.uk/
Simply Direct	www.simplydirect.co.uk/sd_trav.htm
SMS	www.travelinsurance-sms.co.uk/
SoreEyes – Insurance Quotes	www.soreeyes.co.uk/
SRI's Travel Medical Plans	www.specialtyrisk.com/travel.htm
St James Travel	www.stjamestravel.co.uk/

STA Travel	www.statravel.co.uk/
TFG Global Travel Insurance	www.globaltravelinsurance.com/
TIA Travel Insurance	www.travelinsurers.com/
Travel Insurance Club Ltd	www.travelinsuranceclub.co.uk/
Travel Insurance Services	www.travelinsure.com/
Under The Sun Travel Insurance	www.underthesun.co.uk/
West Pennine Insurance	www.westpennine.co.uk/
Worldcare Travel Insurance	www.worldcare.com.au/
Worldcover Direct Limited	www.worldcover.com/
Worldwide Travel Insurance	www.worldwideinsure.com/